Creative Pr

Solving

Level 1

This series is available in print or eBook form.

Level 1 • Level 2

Written by

Carla Fonseca

© 2019
THE CRITICAL THINKING CO.™
www.CriticalThinking.com
Phone: 800-458-4849 • Fax: 541-756-1758
1991 Sherman Ave., Suite 200 • North Bend • OR 97459
ISBN 978-1-60144-957-3

Printed in the United States of America by McNaughton & Gunn, Inc., Saline, MI (Aug. 2019)

Table of Contents

About This Book iii

1. **The Magic Pencil** 1
   Use creative thinking to draw a way to fix a situation.

2. **The Creature Factory** 18
   Draw a creature with the best survival features to survive in a unique habitat on an imaginary planet.

3. **Superheroes and Super Powers** 35
   Choose special powers to help in an emergency.

4. **Alien Designer** 61
   Use creative thinking to draw a design to fit the very specific needs of an alien.

5. **The Inventor** 82
   Use creative thinking to find a solution to someone's problem.

6. **The Crisis Specialist** 105
   Time is very short in emergencies. You must decide the order of the steps to take to help in an emergency.

7. **The Best Tool** 122
   Choose the best tool to help in a situation.

8. **The Enigma*** 139
   Use your imagination to discover the enigmas.

9. **The Mind Ride** 159
   Shut your eyes and imagine you are a character in a story.

Super Challenge

10. **2-D and 3-D Figures and Shading** 174
    Have fun playing with 2-D and 3-D figures.

11. **Play With Mechanisms** 198
    A mechanism is a system of parts that work together in a machine.

About This Book

Imagine and Become a Super Thinker!

Creative problem solving requires more than just knowledge and thinking. Creative problem solving is the process of independently creating a solution. Numerous studies, including ones from the US Department of Education, World Economic Forum, and Bloomberg indicate that tomorrow's jobs will demand creative problem solving skills. Imagination is unlimited power. Someone who has a good imagination can create what does not yet exist.

This book provides educators with fun, highly engaging problems for students' to practice creative problem solving. Students have to evaluate the problem to come up with a workable solution. If a student does not like to draw or cannot write, verbal explanations can be given. Verbal discussions can be a good classroom activity. The challenges will have to be read to younger students. There are no right or wrong solutions, but students should be able to rationally explain why they their solution will work.

1. The Magic Pencil

Use creative thinking to draw a way to fix a situation.

Example: Dog on a Roof

Use your magic pencil to draw a way to save a character from danger or to help the character get what she or he wants.

The dog seems to be jumping from the roof. Use your magic pencil to draw a solution for this dog.

Possible Solutions

1. Add a slide.

2. Put up a fence.

3. Change the dog to a reindeer.

4. Use a rescue helicopter.

Challenge 1: Shark Alert

Alex seems to be swimming with a shark. Use your magic pencil to keep Alex safe from danger.

Challenge 2: Save The Ant!

A shoe is about to crush the ant. Use your magic pencil to make the ant safe.

Challenge 3: Cake in Danger!

The boy wants to eat the piece of cake. Use your magic pencil to save the cake from being eaten.

Challenge 4: Help the Hungry

Ana wants to eat a coconut, but she cannot reach it. Use your magic pencil to help her get it without using a ladder.

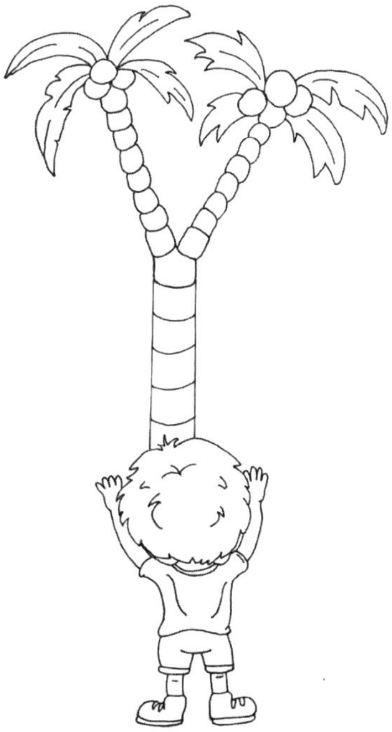

Challenge 5: Dinner Is Almost Ready

The man cannot pull the fish up. Use your magic pencil to add something to the drawing that can help him catch the fish.

Challenge 6: Wake-Up Call

The girl is about to wake up her brother. Keep it from happening with your magic pencil.

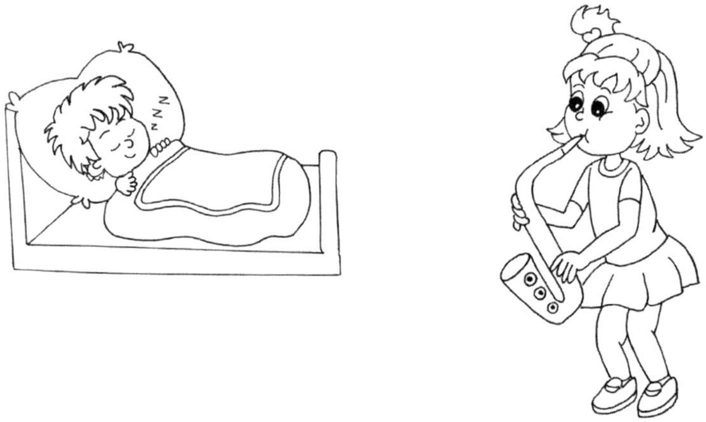

Challenge 7: Scattered Coins

Sofia hides a lot of coins in the sand to play treasure hunt. But they were her brother's savings, and he wants them back. Use your magic pencil to help her collect all the coins easily.

Challenge 8: Fix the Story

The hare is about to win the race with the turtle. Use your magic pencil to help the turtle have a better chance of winning.

Challenge 9: Labyrinth* Search

Billy lost his cap inside a big labyrinth. Use you magic pencil to help him find it, so he does not have to spend so much time running around.

*maze

Challenge 10: Falling Sloth

The branch broke and the sloth is falling to the ground. Save it with your magic pencil.

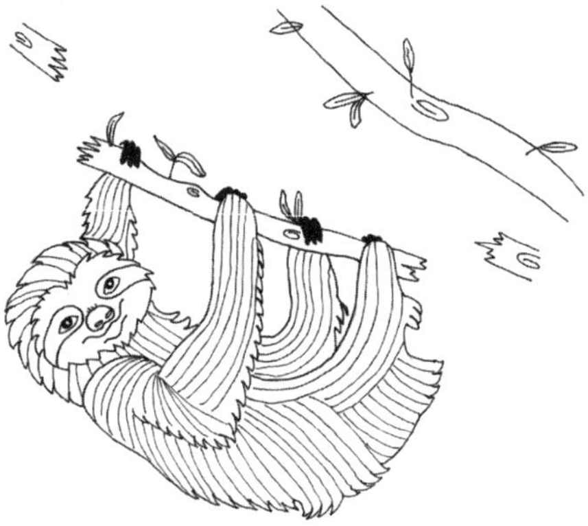

Challenge 11: Aggressive Bee

The bee is going to sting the boy. Use your magic pencil to draw a solution that does not cause harm to the boy.

Challenge 12: The Last Call?

Oops! The phone is about to fall into the toilet. Use your magic pencil to prevent it from happening.

Challenge 13: Big Splash

Lisa is about to do a belly flop in the pool. Use your magic pencil to help her make a soft landing.

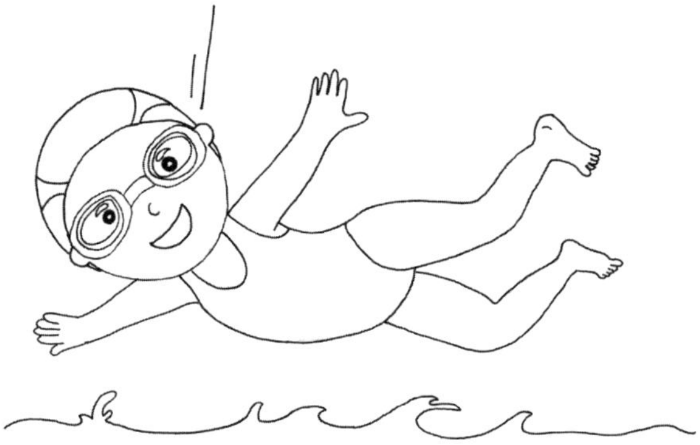

Challenge 14: Locked Car

Mrs. Fields left the car key inside her locked car. Use your magic pencil to help her get inside the car.

Challenge 15: Goal?

The goalkeeper is trying to stop a goal. Use your magic pencil to add something to keep it from happening.

Challenge 16: Annoying Smoke

Naomi is feeling sick from the smoke in the air outside. Use your magic pencil to help her feel better.

Challenge 17: Hole in the Bag

Mrs. Martin does not know she is dropping items as she walks. Use your magic pencil to help her avoid losing things.

Challenge 18: Pet Earthworm

The earthworm, about to be eaten below, is a special pet of the fisherman's son. He just realized his father used it by mistake. Use your magic pencil to help the earthworm before it is too late.

Challenge 19: Lightning, Camera...Action

Lightning is going to strike the umbrella. Use your magic pencil to keep the man safe.

Challenge 20: Hot! Hot!

Little Nicole is about to touch a very hot cup. Use your magic pencil to prevent her getting burned.

Challenge 21: Tsunami

A big wave is about to go over the house. Use your magic pencil to save the house from getting damaged.

Challenge 22: An Ugly Kiss

The cow is going to lick Molly's face. Use your magic pencil to prevent this.

Challenge 23: Low Bridge

Sylvia is paddling down the river and comes upon a very low bridge. Use your magic pencil to draw a solution so she can continue down the river.

Challenge 24: Big Bully

Scott was on his way to class when he ran in to the big school bully. Use your magic pencil to draw a way to protect him from the bully.

Challenge 25: The Way Home

The sheep are lost. Use your magic pencil to help them find their way back to the farm.

Challenge 26: Oh, Oh A Bear!

You are inside a bear's cave. The hungry mother bear and her baby are outside. Use your magic pencil to help you get out of the cave to avoid the danger.

Challenge 27: Endangered Tree

The logger wants to cut a very special tree. Use your magic pencil to save the tree.

Challenge 28: Monster?

Joel is scared of the monster. Use your magic pencil to make him unafraid.

2. The Creature Factory

Draw a creature with the best survival features to survive in a unique habitat on an imaginary planet.

Example: Planet Swamp

Planet Swamp is very dark and swampy. The soil is muddy. There are many flies, mosquitoes, and insects. Predators, such as the alligator below, find it difficult to be sneaky, because their footsteps make splashing sounds in the mud. They are very thin because they don't get enough to eat.

Draw the creature you think could survive in this habitat. What is the name of the new creature? Why do you think it would survive on planet Swamp?

Possible Answer

It would have snake eyes to see better in the dark, rabbit ears to hear the splashes of predators, and a frog tongue to eat insects.

The Bunny Froggy

Challenge 1: Planet Wet

On planet Wet, it rains every day. The ground is soft as a sponge and sinks when you step on it. There is foam in the air, which makes it difficult to see what is hidden in it. The bottom layer is water that lacks oxygen. It is overcrowded with hungry fish. On the seabed there are many thorny corals.

Draw the creature you think could survive in this habitat. What is the name of the new creature? Why do you think it would survive on planet Wet?

Challenge 2: Planet Rollers

Planet Rollers is flat and has two rollers, one at each end of the planet. One roller crushes everything on the ground. The other one provides new, fresh ground. The ground is constantly moving. If something sleeps longer than it should, it could wake up inside the roller. Below the ground there are stones and hot lava.

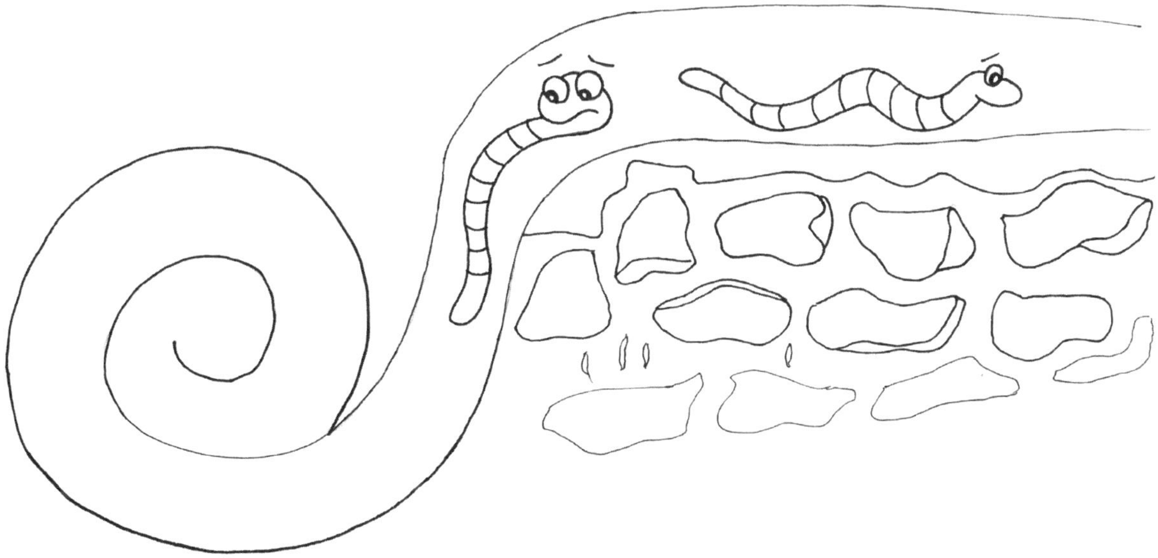

Draw the creature you think could survive in this habitat. What is the name of the new creature? Why do you think it would survive on planet Rollers?

____

____

____

____

Challenge 3: Planet Sharp

Planet Sharp has sharp rocks everywhere. The sky and ground can tear and scratch everything. During the rainy season, water gets stuck at the lowest points, forming small pools where moss and insects live until the dry season arrives.

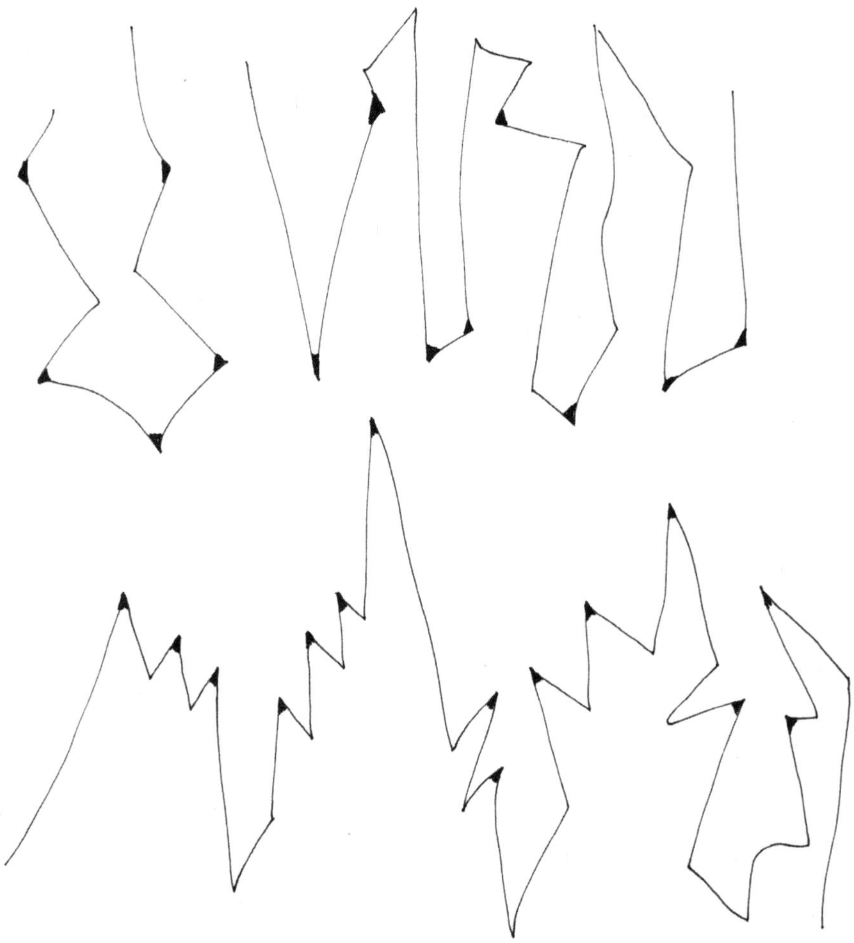

Draw the creature you think could survive in this habitat. What is the name of the new creature? Why do you think it would survive on planet Sharp?

Challenge 4: Planet Holes

On planet Holes, the holes appear and disappear at any time by magic. Some are deep and others small. Walking there is a dangerous adventure. The wind is very strong, making it difficult to fly or stand upright. The planet is abundant in vegetables such as carrots and potatoes.

Draw the creature you think could survive in this habitat. What is the name of the new creature? Why do you think it would survive on planet Holes?

Challenge 5: Planet Branches

The floor of planet Branches is covered with toxic, hot lava. A few yards from the ground is an abundant layer of branches. Among the branches are climbing plants that move like snakes to hold onto whatever they find in their path. It is hard to breathe because the air is very hot and scarce. Among the branches are many round fruits with very hard shells.

Draw the creature you think could survive in this habitat. What is the name of the new creature? Why do you think it would survive on planet Branches?

Challenge 6: Planet Heavy Rain

It rains coconuts on planet Heavy Rain. The clouds are palm trees hanging all over the planet. There are mountains of coconuts on the ground that makes it difficult to walk, because they are very unstable.

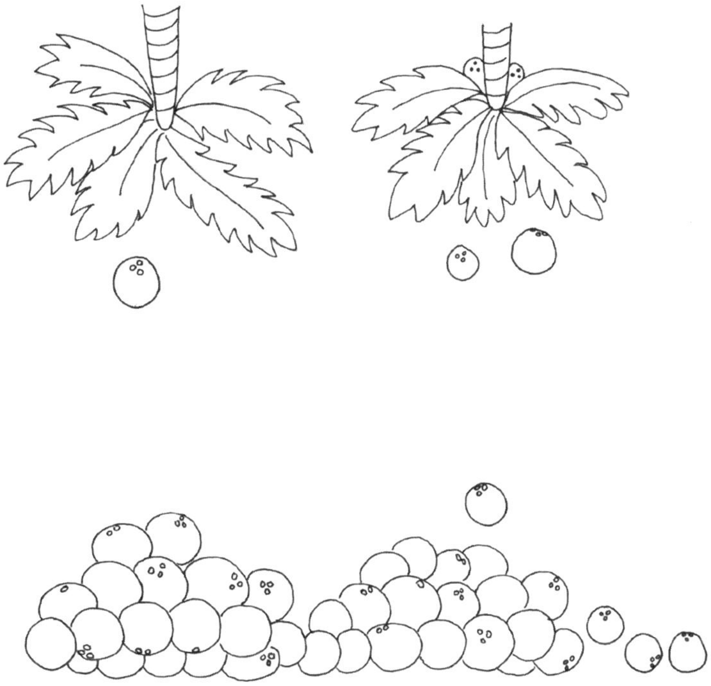

Draw the creature you think could survive in this habitat. What is the name of the new creature? Why do you think it would survive on planet Heavy Rain?

Challenge 7: Planet Vacuum

The sky is a big vacuum cleaner on planet Vacuum. The trees start loosing leaves as they grow so they do not grow very large. The fruit does not have time to grow big, because they are vacuumed up when they are still green.

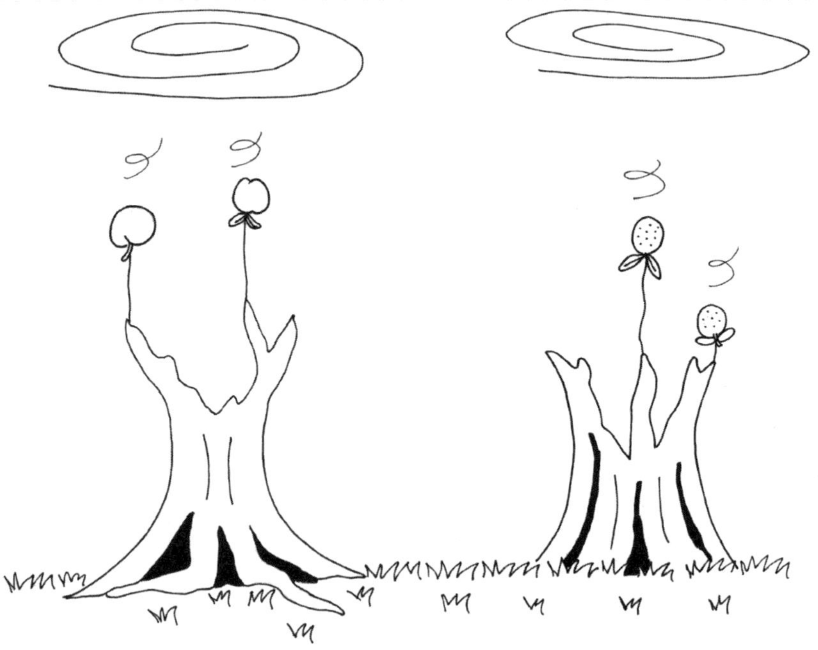

Draw the creature you think could survive in this habitat. What is the name of the new creature? Why do you think it would survive on planet Vacuum?

Challenge 8: Planet Garbage

Planet Garbage is where all the other planets send their garbage. At any time, a spaceship can drop garbage any place. There are trash compactors all over the ground, so the garbage uses less space. It smells awful.

Draw the creature you think could survive in this habitat. What is the name of the new creature? Why do you think it would survive on planet Garbage?

Challenge 9: Planet Extreme Weather

On planet Extreme Weather, the mornings are very hot and dry. The nights are cold and snowy. There are cacti all over.

Draw the creature you think could survive in this habitat. What is the name of the new creature? Why do you think it would survive on planet Extreme Weather?

Challenge 10: The Circle Of Life

You made up nine creatures that could live in a unique habitat on an imaginary planet. Now answer the following questions. You can draw the creatures or write their names.

1. Who is the strongest?

2. Who is the weakest?

3. If they all live on the same planet, how will they interact?

4. Who will eat who?

5. Which creatures can live in the same habitat? What is the best way to represent how they all live in Together land?

Habitat Challenge

Draw the habitat in which a special creature has the best chances of surviving.

Habitat Challenge 1: Long-Tongue Giraffe

This giraffe has long legs and a very short neck. It has a long tongue like a butterfly. The horns are strong and are used to fight each other, but can get stuck together.

In the picture, draw the habitat where the long-tongue giraffe is a dominant predator and the food you think it can eat. What is the name of the planet? Why do you think it would survive well in this habitat?

Habitat Challenge 2: Giant Eggshell

This creature has an eggshell bottom. It is very fragile. It can crack if it falls on something hard. All the other creatures where the Giant Eggshell lives fear it.

In the picture, draw the habitat where the giant eggshell is a dominant predator and the food you think it can eat. What is the name of the planet? Why do you think it would survive well in this habitat?

Habitat Challenge 3: Suction Cup Blanket

This creature is like a blanket. It has suction cups to move.

In the picture, draw the habitat where the suction cup blanket is a dominant predator and the food you think it can eat. What is the name of the planet? Why do you think it would survive well in this habitat?

Habitat Challenge 4: Suck-Up Giant

This creature has a mouth like a vacuum cleaner. It has no eyes. His legs are short, and he is very heavy.

In the picture, draw the habitat where the suck-up giant is a dominant predator and the food you think it can eat. What is the name of the planet? Why do you think it would survive well in this habitat?

Habitat Challenge 5: Moving Umbrella

This creature has leaves on some parts of its body. Its hair looks like a very thin umbrella. It has long, agile legs and arms.

In the picture, draw the habitat where the moving umbrella is a dominant predator and the food you think it can eat. What is the name of the planet? Why do you think it would survive well in this habitat?

3. Superheroes and Super Powers

Choose special powers to help in an emergency.

Example: The Class Floods

A river near your school has risen so high that it has entered your classroom. The water is at the same level as the seat of your chair. Twenty classmates are standing on the chairs, and the water is still coming in.

Choose a super power below to help you save your classmates.

Vaporizer

Your microwave eyes heat the water in an instant vaporizing it

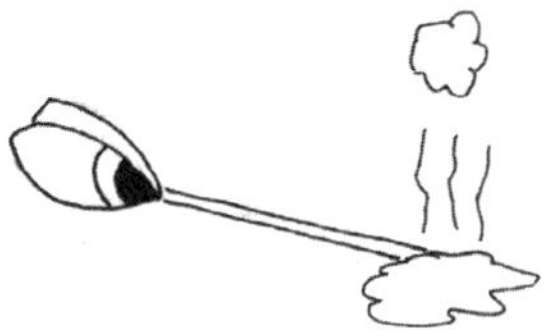

Super Bubble

You can make a bubble in which some of the children can float.

Cool

Your breath freezes the water around you.

Canoe Shoes

You can make shoes become small canoes.

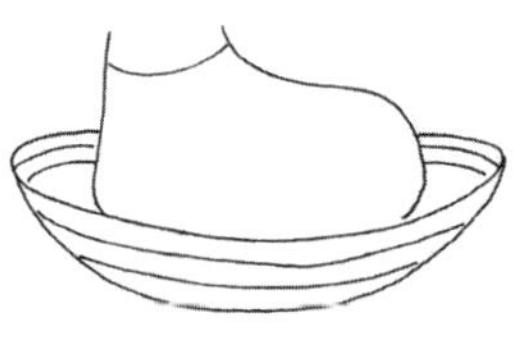

Which super power did you choose? Why? Why didn't you choose the others?

I would choose the power to freeze the water. The kids can stay still until they are rescued or walk over the frozen water if it is solid and safe. I would not vaporize the water because the heated water and the vapor could burn. I would not use the bubble because it cannot save many children at the same time. The canoe shoes can be a risky choice, because it is not known if they are easy to handle and if more water can come in like a big wave.

What is a different super power that could be helpful?

A power that can make the water disappear would be a good choice. It would save all the kids and the building from damage.

Team Work

You are now the head of the mission to rescue all the people trapped inside the flooded school. You still have your special power.

Choose two superheroes below to help you save all the people. Explain your plan.

Glue: He throws Superglue to glue heavy things to dry surfaces.

Stingray: She becomes a big, strong stingray that moves fast in water.

Suction: He suctions anything from his feet and throws it far away.

The Wizard: Whatever his coat covers, it moves somewhere else.

I would choose the wizard and the glue. I would go from class to class freezing the water. The wizard will make the people disappear by covering them with his coat one at a time and sending them to a safe place. Glue can stick chairs and tables high on the wall. The people will be above the water while the wizard sends them to a safer place.

Challenge 1: Emergency Landing

A plane is making an emergency landing in the park. Your sister is flying a kite, and the wind makes the kite string wrap around her feet. Now the plane's engine is pulling the kite in. Your sister is in danger. You are holding her hands but they are slipping.

Choose a super power below to help you save your sister.

Elastic

You can stretch your hand several yards.

Super Gum

Your body is a very sticky gum.

Mega Strong

You can lift a refrigerator.

Donut Arms

Your arms can form the shape of a donut and hold what is inside very strongly.

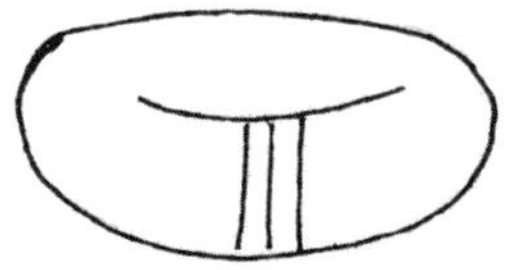

Which super power did you choose? Why? Why didn't you choose the others?

What is a different super power that could be helpful?

Team Work

You are now the head of the mission to save other people on the ground from the plane's emergency landing. You still have your special power.

Choose two superheroes below to help you. Explain your plan.

Photoshop: He can select and move things as big as a car from the real world.

Stretch Hair: A bunch of her hair gets very long and strong as a steel rope.

Gum Pumps: He can make very big, unbreakable chewing gum pump.

Air Blower: Her weapon blows super-fast air

Challenge 2: Avalanche

Two buses are on a field trip. Your bus arrives first. Five of your classmates get out and start exploring the area. The second bus is just arriving, when suddenly one of your friends yells "avalanche!" Everyone looks at the mountain, and they see a huge amount of snow that will soon fall on the buses and the people around it.

Choose a super power below to help you save all the people.

Laser Eyes

Your eyes can blow up stones and giant mountains with just a glance.

Elastic Stomach

Your stomach can stretch hundreds of yards forming an elastic barrier for up to twenty minutes.

Fly

You have the power to fly and the strength of an elephant.

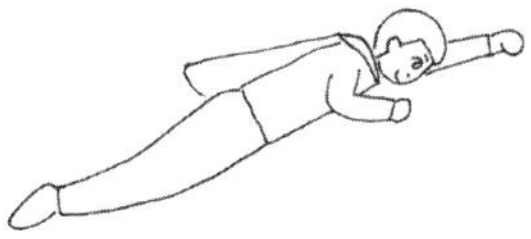

Defrost

Your breath can melt a lot of ice.

Which super power did you choose? Why? Why didn't you choose the others?

What is a different super power that could be helpful?

Team Work

The avalanche is also falling in another part of the mountain and it is about to fall on a town nearby. You are now the head of the mission to save the town. You still have your special power.

Choose two superheroes below to help you save the town. Explain your plan.

Speedy: He is the fastest man on Earth.

Writing Glasses: Her glasses can write messages in the sky.

Stomp: When he stomps the ground, he makes big holes.

Temperature Controller: She can make the weather colder or hotter.

Challenge 3: Trapped in an Elevator

There is a general electricity failure in the town. You are trapped in an elevator with three children. It is dark and hot. The atmosphere is very heavy, as if it lacks oxygen.

Choose a super power below to get everyone safely out of the elevator.

Metamorfo

All the people you touch transform into an ant and back again to a person after a few minutes.

Blue Lantern

Your ring lights up like a blue lantern.

Super Breath

Your breath is cold oxygen.

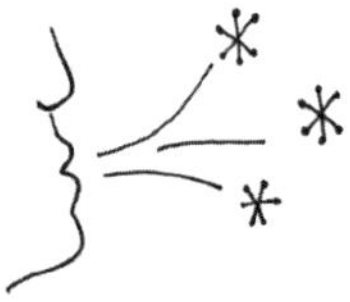

Melter

Your hand can melt metal.

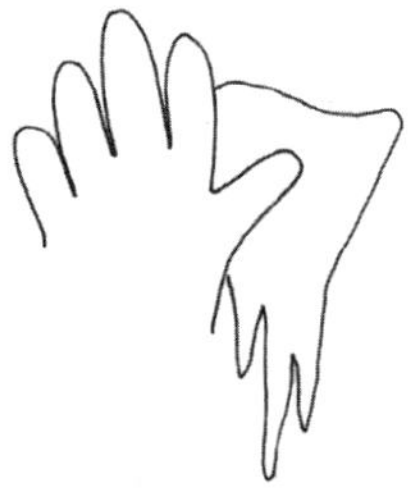

Which super power did you choose? Why? Why didn't you choose the others?

What is a different super power that could be helpful?

Team Work

There is chaos in the town because of the long electricity failure. You are now the head of the mission to restore order. You still have your special power.

Choose two superheroes below to help you restore order to the town. Explain your plan.

Lightning: He throws lightning from his ears.

Glower: He glows in the dark.

Copy Machine: She can copy what she scans with her eyes and the duplicates last for an hour.

Size Changer: She can make things or people smaller or larger.

Challenge 4: Lost in the Crowd

Your family is at a concert with a lot of people. Suddenly lightning and thunder announce a storm is about to begin. People are starting to be nervous. Your parents realize that your younger brother has been lost among the people. You must think of a way to help them find him soon.

Choose a super power below to help you find your brother.

Dog Nose

Your nose allows you to identify different scents in the air, as if you were a tracking dog,

Megaphone Voice

Your voice sounds very loud and spreads several yards away.

Telescopic Eyes

You can see very far.

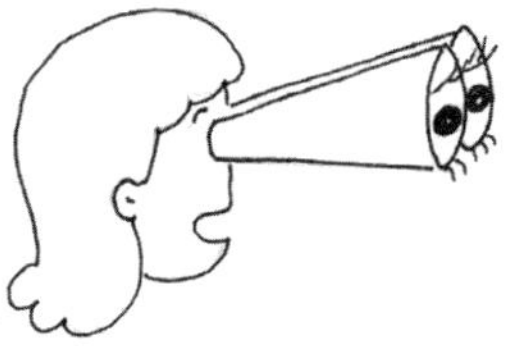

Helicopter

There are propellers on your head that allow you to fly like a helicopter.

Which super power did you choose? Why? Why didn't you choose the others?

What is a different super power that could be helpful?

Team Work

Lightning strikes the ground near the crowd, and they all start running. You are now the head of the mission to control the crowd. You still have your super power.

Choose two superheroes below to help you control the crowd. Explain your plan.

Transporter Cloud: She transforms in to a cloud which can move a large group of people from one place to another.

Mentalist: He can make people do what he orders.

Rainbow Shadow: She can draw a rainbow in the sky. All who are below it are covered by a protective shadow.

Sun Caress: He projects an image of the sun in the sky and makes people below it feel like they are under the sun.

Challenge 5: Lost in the Woods

You are on a school trip. It is getting dark and you will soon be leaving on the bus. You see a squirrel and follow it. Then you fall down a small hill. You are fine, but you also notice that you have been running for some time, and you are now lost. You start screaming and walking around. You cannot hear anyone calling you. The night is getting darker and colder.

Choose a super power below to help you find your way back to the bus.

Fluorescent Head

Your head becomes very bright in the dark.

Hair Shelter

Your hair becomes a very safe shelter. It will protect you from animals and cold.

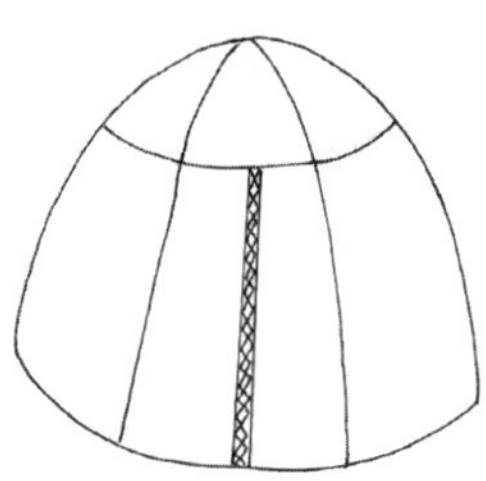

Fire Finger

Your finger can make fire.

Owl

You become a night owl for ten minutes.

Which super power did you choose? Why? Why didn't you choose the others?

____

____

____

____

What is a different super power that could be helpful?

____

Team Work

Your teachers have found you, but there is another girl missing. You are now the head of the rescue mission searching for that lost girl. You still have your super power.

Choose two superheroes below to help you find the lost girl. Explain your plan.

Thermic Vision: He can see hot objects in the dark as if they were glowing.

Tree Talker: She can communicate with trees.

Super Lamp: She can illuminate a whole town for an hour.

Ultrasound: He can hear low sounds as if they were loud.

____

____

____

____

____

Challenge 6: Horse Stampede

You are walking near a barn when suddenly you feel the ground move. You turn and see a group of horses coming at you in a stampede.

Choose a super power below to save yourself from the stampede.

High Jumper

You can jump twice your size as many times as you want

Fast Cheetah

You can run fast, like a cheetah.

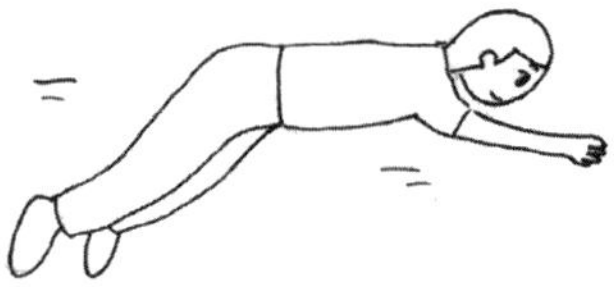

Ultra Driller

Your feet roll in a high-speed motion that can make an instant hole in the ground.

Roaring Sound

You can make a powerfully loud sound which can scare away anything.

Which super power did you choose? Why? Why didn't you choose the others?

____

____

____

____

____

What is a different super power that could be helpful?

____

Team Work

You are now the head of the mission to stop the stampeding horses. You still have your super power.

Choose two superheroes below to help you stop the stampede. Explain your plan.

Mind Mover: She can move one object at a time with the power of her mind.

Seed Planter: He has ultra-fast growth seeds.

Animal Talker: He can communicate with animals.

Net Hair: Her hair grows as a big, strong net.

____

____

____

____

____

Challenge 7: Trapped in an Ice Hole

You are walking through the forest snow starts to fall very hard. You decide to go home, but you can't see very well because of the snow and wind. Then you fall in to a deep ice hole. You are surrounded by a slippery surface very far from the top of the hole.

Choose a super power below to help you get out of the ice hole.

Stretch Leg

You have a leg that stretches several yards.

Air Sprayer

Your feet make a powerful spray of air.

Ice Maker

You can make a lot of ice from your hand.

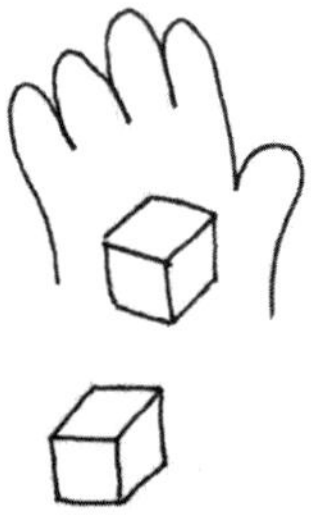

Ice Climber Hand

You have one hand that has picks to help climb.

Which super power did you choose? Why? Why didn't you choose the others?

What is a different super power that could be helpful?

Team Work

You are now out of the hole. The weather is getting worse, and there are many people that have not been able to return home. You are the head of the rescue mission for the people trapped in the snow. You still have your special power.

Choose two superheroes below to help you rescue the people trapped in the snow. Explain your plan.

Teleporter: He can teleport two persons anywhere.

Foot Printer: He can make fresh foot prints luminous.

Thermic Bubble: She can make bubbles that are warm inside.

Camera Vision: She can think of different places and view them as if through a camera.

Challenge 8: Big Wave

You and your sisters are playing in the sand on the seashore. Suddenly you see a BIG wave is about to burst on the beach.

Choose a super power below to save you and your sisters from the big wave.

Mr. Sandman

A lot of sand comes out of your feet, forming the shape you want.

Lord of the Dolphins

You can mentally control dolphins.

Super Surfboard

It allows you to surf like a pro even if you are just an amateur.

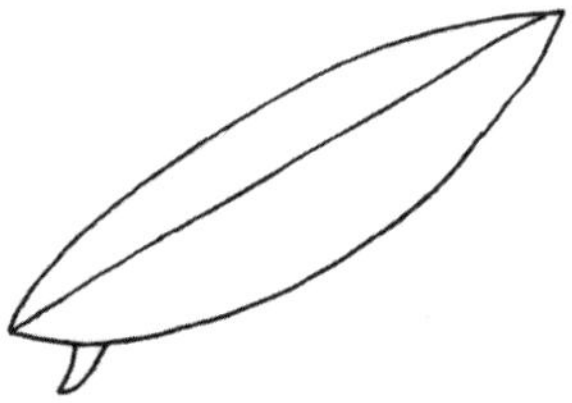

Bucket Swallower

It swallows all the water that fits in the bucket and continues doing it.

Which super power did you choose? Why? Why didn't you choose the others?

____

____

____

____

____

What is a different super power that could be helpful?

____

Team Work

You are now head of the mission to save all the people from a tsunami that will soon hit the beach. You still have your special power.

Choose two superheroes below to help you save the people from the tsunami. Explain your plan.

Clock Slower: She makes time go in slow motion for two minutes.

The Drawer: He can draw objects and make them appear.

The Wall: She can build air walls in a blink.

Time Traveler: She can travel five minutes in the past.

____

____

____

____

Top Super Powers

There are super powers that are good for many different tasks. Some super powers are useful only for particular situations.

Which are the top five super powers listed in all the challenges?

1. ____________________
2. ____________________
3. ____________________
4. ____________________
5. ____________________

Explain why each of these super powers is in the top five.

____

____

____

____

____

Which five super powers listed in all the challenges are useless?

1. ____________________
2. ____________________
3. ____________________
4. ____________________
5. ____________________

Explain why each of these super powers is useless.

Which two super powers are the best combination? Explain why.

Villain Challenge

Think of a villain who could beat each superhero.

Villain Challenge 1: Honeybear

This superhero's legs are similar to lizard legs. It climbs trees and walks very fast. It carries a pot of very sticky honey. It refills by magic. The superhero uses its trunk to spray the honey on trees or the ground so his enemies have a hard time moving. They also wonder where the closest shower is to be able to clean themselves.

What super powers would a villain need to beat the hero? What is the villain's name? (If you want, draw your villain on a separate sheet of paper.)

Villain Challenge 2: Hair Tornado

This superhero has an infinite amount of hair and is not afraid of using it. The tornados of hair can roll the strongest villain and make him dizzy.

What super powers would a villain need to beat the hero? What is the villain's name? (If you want, draw your villain on a separate sheet of paper.)

Villain Challenge 3: Teeth Launcher

This flying shark superhero shoots teeth with a potion that tranquilizes. The villains fall asleep and wake up in jail.

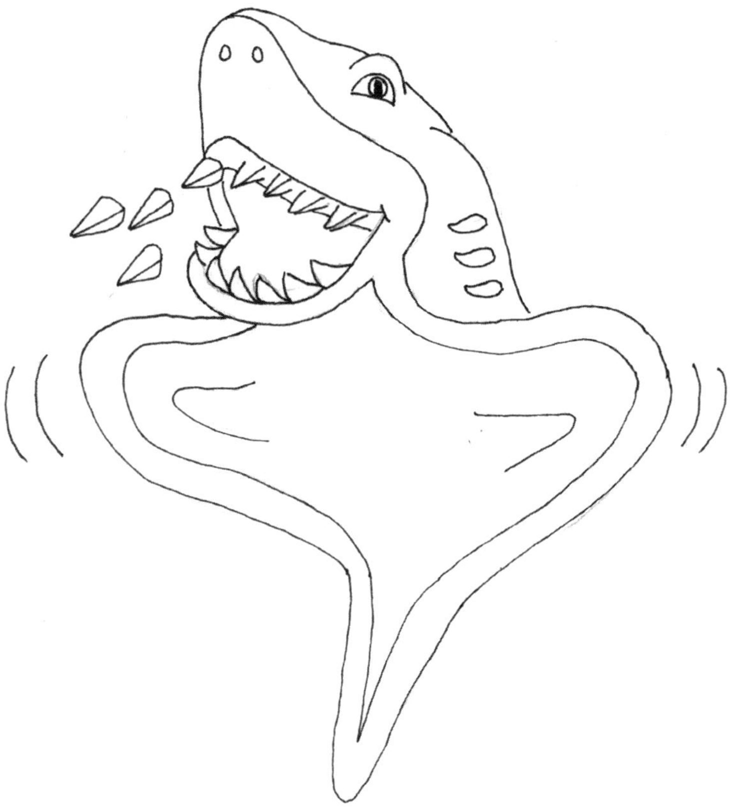

What super powers would a villain need to beat the hero? What is the villain's name? (If you want, draw your villain on a separate sheet of paper.)

Villain Challenge 4: Mud Ball

The mud ball superhero is big and fast and rolls over the villains or their weapons.

What super powers would a villain need to beat the hero? What is the villain's name? (If you want, draw your villain on a separate sheet of paper.)

Villain Challenge 5: The Invisible Ultra Glue

This is an invisible superhero. It moves very fast and sprays ultra glue. The villains try to move and find theirselves glued to a surface. Sometimes they get glued by their hair, at other times by their shoes or hands.

There is no picture, because it is invisible all the time and so is its glue.

What super powers would a villain need to beat the hero? What is the villain's name? (If you want, draw your villain on a separate sheet of paper.)

____

____

____

____

____

____

4. Alien Designer

Use creative thinking to draw a design to fit the very specific needs of an alien.

Example: A Chair for Willy

An alien, very similar to a snowman, just entered your office. His name is Willy. His legs are a pair of sticks that allow him to walk. You ask him to sit down, but he tells you he finds chairs very uncomfortable. That is why he came to see you. He needs you to design a chair that fits his needs. He has a hard time sitting because his legs are short and do not have knees that bend. When he comes to a low chair, his rounded shape makes him roll to the floor. He wants to be able to rest his legs and his spine on a special chair.

Design a chair for Willy.

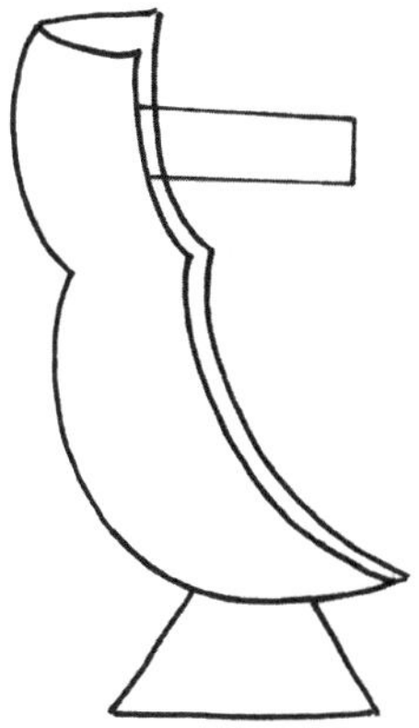

Why do you think it will work?

I designed a low chair because Willy's feet are small. The chair is rounded to stop him from rolling to the sides. He can rest his back in the upper part of the chair. It is also rounded. The place to rest the arms is up in the chair where his arms start because he has no elbows.

Challenge 1: Toothbrush for an Alien Mouth

An alien, resembling a big insect, comes to your office. It seems to be a "she" because her eyelashes are long. Her mouth looks like a straw and she talks like a person who can barely open her lips, "I heard you are a spectacular designer. I want you to design a brush to help me wash my teeth."

You ask her to open the mouth. Now you understand her concern. You notice hundreds of teeth that go from the lips down to the end of the straw-shaped mouth. You are relieved that you are her designer. It must be impossible to be her dentist. You look at her hands and realize you have to come up with an idea for the brush handle, too. Those short insect legs will not help her grab a regular brush.

Design a toothbrush for the alien.

Why do you think it will work?

Challenge 2: Bushie's Sweater

The sound of moving leaves lets you know your next customer has arrived. It looks like a bear-tree. He looks so sweet you almost forget how strong he might be. A voice outside the door says, "Hi! This is my son Bushie. I am sorry that I cannot come in. I am afraid I would break your door, your wall, or both. I came to ask you a very special favor. I need you to design a sweater for him. He still does not have many leaves to protect his six branches, and they get very cold at night. I am afraid with winter coming that he will be sneezing all over the place. Every time he sneezes, a lot of his leaves fall down and there you go! Another bald tree for winter! Please design him a sweater and find a way to put it on without hurting his fragile leaves. If you do, I promise I will bring my birds to sing to you in the spring."

Design a sweater for Bushie.

Why do you think it will work?

Challenge 3: Gusin's Eyeglasses

You just finished a phone call with a client and come out to the waiting room to call the next one. You find a caterpillar reading a magazine. It seems to be comfortable, because eight of its legs are on the floor. It has thirty eyes, located in the front, side, and behind its head. It is reading with some of them. Others, you are not sure how many, are looking directly at you. It approaches with two of its feet extended. "Hello. I am Gusin. I need eyeglasses, and I have not being able to find what I need. I need to see through all of my eyes to take care of my predators, to move, and to look for food. I need the same prescription glasses for all thirty eyes. Can you help me? Please design eyeglasses that can fit my needs."

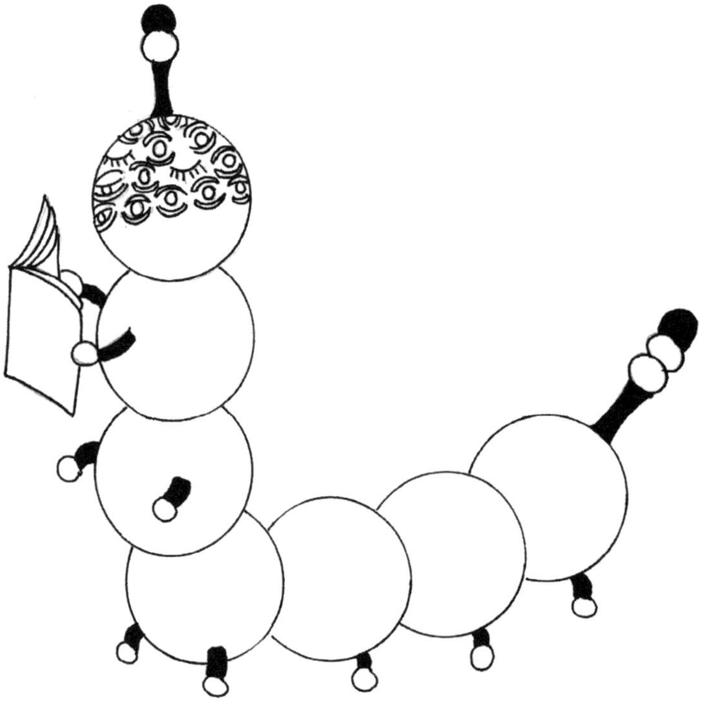

Design eyeglasses for Gusin.

Why do you think they will work?

Challenge 4: Robby's Gift

Robby comes to your office crying. He puts a bag on your desk. You try to calm him down but he just makes robotic noises. They sound like a sad trumpet and a car horn. He tells you, "tuturututu…. I want ……tuturututu… a very special gift for my mom….tuturutuupiiiiiiiiiiiipp. She cannot grab regular mugs… Our fingers…. tuturutuupiiiiiiiiiiiiiiipptuturutupiiiiiiiiiiiiiiiiiiiiiiiiiiiiiip.

He keeps crying. Therefore you open the bag and find a mug with the picture of Robby on it. You draw his hand on a piece of paper and ask him to come back later. You tell him you will think of a solution for his problem.

Robby's Hand

What is Robby's problem?

____

____

____

____

____

____

Design a solution for him.

Why do you think it will work?

Challenge 5: Gamer R85

Your last client told R85 to come see you. R85 is a young robotic alien. Its hands are designed to type. It has two fingers in each hand which can move up and down and fold in the middle. It loves video games but finds the controller very uncomfortable. It wants you to design a controller fitted for it. R85 says it cannot pay you, but it will include a free ad for your designer office when it becomes a famous gamer.

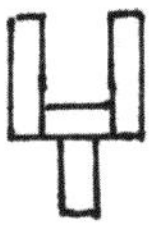

R85's Hand

Design R85's controller.

Why do you think it will work?

Challenge 6: Bubbly's Home

Bubbly sent you a picture with this message. "My friends told me you are an amazing designer. I sent you a picture of my home because I have a problem. My home gets dirty very often. There are food leftovers floating around the water. I love when my house is clean, and the water has no color at all. But when days pass by, the water turns to the orange color of my food. I cannot smell it, but I do have eyes. I do not want to continue swimming in the blurry fluid. To clean my house, I usually need a lot of help. I would like a home that is easier to clean. I would like a small place inside it where I can stay while the old water drains out and the clean water comes in. Please design a new home for me. I am sure it will become a big seller. Not to mention how much you can earn with the whale version!"

Design a home for fish. It can have parts outside the tank, but Bubbly cannot swim outside of the tank.

Why do you think it will work?

Challenge 7: Sneaky's Stairs

A very big snake enters your office. You try to be calm and surpass the first impression. "Excuse me for entering without giving previous notice of my arrival," she says. "My name is Sneaky of the Southern Jungles. I just moved to the city. My friend Viper Piper convinced me to buy a spectacular two-story house from a different species. She told me I could hire a decorator later to make all the arrangements. But I need more than a decorator to fit the house for my needs. I find the stairs to be very difficult to climb. I want you to design an easier way to go up to the second floor. But I must tell you I absolutely hate elevators, and electric stairs hurt my skin." You try to open your mouth for the first time since she arrived, but she continues. "Please send me a draft with your idea F.A.A.S. (Fast As A Snake). And now I must leave for I am late for my massage. Have a good day!"

Redesign the stairs, or design an accessory or system for Sneaky to go up to the second floor.

Why do you think it will work?

Challenge 8: Noos's Spoon

You are eating a snack in your desk when suddenly you hear a flip-flop sound. You lift your head and see nothing. All of a sudden, three moving eyes appear in front of you. You jump back. The eyes disappear below your desk. You look behind the desk and find a small creature. "So sorrrry," it says. "I am Noos." You tell it that you were about to finish your snack and offer it something to eat. Noos says, "I do not have teeth. I just eat soft food." You offer it a yogurt in a bowl. It sinks his face in to the bowl and eats all of it. Then he tells you, "I have always wanted to be able to use a spoon. I am usually very neat, and I want to be able to eat without making a mess. Please design a spoon for me."

Design a spoon for Noos.

Why do you think it will work?

Challenge 9: Rosie's Back Pain

Rosie has an injury to her back. She feels pain when she walks. She thinks some support for her belly will help her. "But," she adds, "you must know my petals are very delicate. They make me the prettiest flower, after all. I am not saying they are not strong, but if you are thinking of straps, please take care of my petals. My lower part, however, is made of hard skin. Please design a belly support for me."

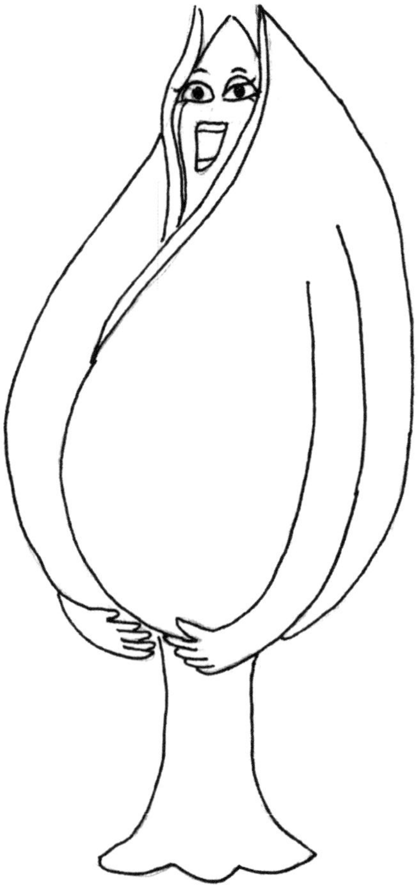

Design the belly support for Rosie.

Why do you think it will work?

5. The Inventor

Use creative thinking to find a solution to someone's problem.

Example: Toothbrush Cup

Lily has a problem. The bottom of the glass where she puts her toothbrush is very dirty. There is water and toothpaste from the brush that drains in to the glass. Lily thinks the glass is not well designed to keep her brush clean.

Draw or write your possible solutions.

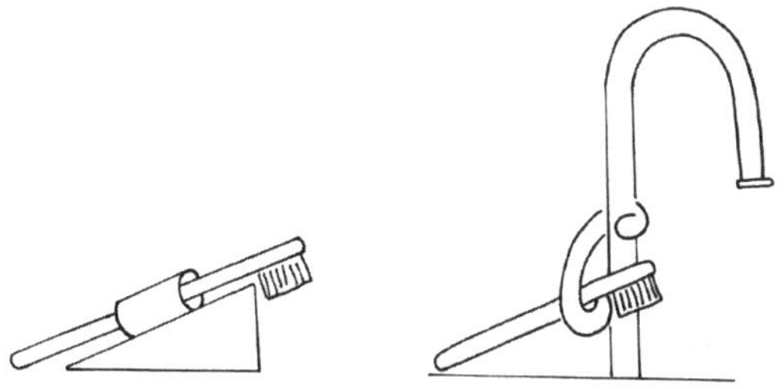

Choose a solution and write Lily a note explaining why you think it would work.

I drew two ideas. I like the triangular holder. It will keep the brush from touching the table, and it can be placed near the faucet to drain. I think a container for the toothbrush will end up getting dirty. I choose to make the toothbrush drain directly on the faucet because it is frequently cleaned.

Challenge 1: Water Tap

Tita uses a wheelchair. She has short arms and cannot turn on the water faucet to wash the dishes. The handle turns clockwise to turn on the faucet. Design a tool to help her turn on the water faucet.

Draw or write your possible solutions.

Choose a solution and write Tita a note explaining why you think it would work.

Challenge 2: Special Silverware

Michael has an injury to both of his hands. He can move his arms, but he cannot move his fingers so he cannot hold anything. He needs you to design special silverware for him to feed himself.

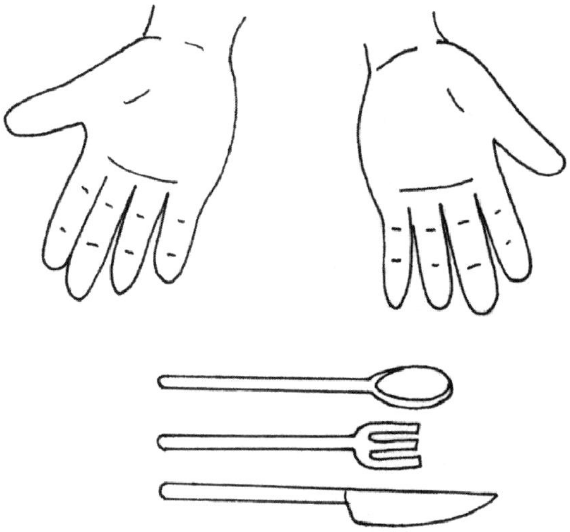

Draw or write your possible solutions.

Choose a solution and write Michael a note explaining why you think it would work.

Challenge 3: Making the Bed

Joanna is a very independent toddler. She wants to make everything by herself. She gets very frustrated when trying to make her bed, because she cannot reach the side of the bed that is next to the wall. She usually gets on top of the pillow to pull the sheets. But when she gets off the bed it ends up looking messy.

Draw your possible solutions and explain how to use them. (Joanna does not read.)

Challenge 4: Sprinkler

Mary usually takes care of her bonsai. She and her family are going away on vacation. The bonsai is very heavy to take it with her. She must figure out a way for it to survive during her absence. She needs an indoor plant sprinkler that gives the right amount of water.

Draw or write your possible solutions.

Choose a solution and write Mary a note explaining why you think it would work.

Challenge 5: The Scratcher

Susan finds it relaxing to be scratched on the back. Her mother used scratch Susan's back to help her go to sleep. Her mother recently had a baby, and she does not have enough time to scratch Susan's back. Susan tried to tape five pencils together to scratch her own back, but it did not work well. It does not feel like nails.

Draw or write your possible solutions.

Choose a solution and write Susan a note explaining why you think it would work.

Challenge 6: The Cramps

Tony is recovering from an injury to his leg. His knee is bandaged, and he cannot flex it. That is why he is getting cramps in his right foot. His cramps make his foot point like a dancer. He feels better when someone helps him put his foot back in a normal position, but when there is no one around, the pain last a long time.

Draw or write your possible solutions.

Choose a solution and write Tony a note explaining why you think it would work.

Challenge 7: Salesman's Bags

A street salesman is selling bags of fruit and vegetables. He always takes three bags in each hand and goes around selling them. In that way he can take different products. When he sells them, he goes back to his truck to get more. He would like to be able to carry more bags with him, because the truck is far. He also would like the product to be at the eye level of a person passing in a car.

Draw or write your possible solutions.

Choose a solution and write the salesman a note explaining why you think it would work.

Challenge 8: Ball Picker Upper

Your friend always asks you to play dodgeball with small plastic coloured balls. You run around the house throwing the balls at each other. The game is very fun until it ends, and you have to pick up all the balls from the floor. It is especially difficult to pick them from under the beds.

Draw or write your possible solutions.

Choose a solution and write your friend a note explaining why you think it would work.

Challenge 9: Small Dog

Your neighbor just adopted a very small dog. He lives in a two-story house. The dog has managed to climb up the stairs, but he cannot go down. The stairs are so big that he falls down and rolls to the ground. When he wants to go down, he starts crying and barking. Your neighbor wants him to be free to go up and down without help.

Draw or write your possible solutions.

Choose a solution and write your neighbor a note explaining why you think it would work.

Challenge 10: Fingernail Biter

Hanna usually bites her nails when she watches TV. She wants to stop doing it, but it is a difficult habit to stop. Help her figure out a solution; either invent something that is similar to a nail that she can bite or a way to prevent her from biting her nails. Please make it comfortable.

Draw or write your possible solutions.

Choose a solution and write Hanna a note explaining why you think it would work.

Challenge 11: Playground for Pets

Daniel has a hamster named Willy. Willy is very bored. Daniel wants to make him a playground reusing materials such as boxes, juice containers, and plastic bottles. Since Daniel is only four years old, he has not been able to make progress with his project.

Make a drawing of a playground for Daniel's pet.

Use boxes, juice containers, and plastic bottles to make a drawing of a game for Willy.

Challenge 12: Water Recycling

Scott's dad showed him the plans of the house they are going to build. Scott is a kid concerned about the environment. He wants you to suggest ways of recycling water inside the house. Think where the soapy water that remains can be reused.

Draw the path that the recycled water would follow in the rectangles below.

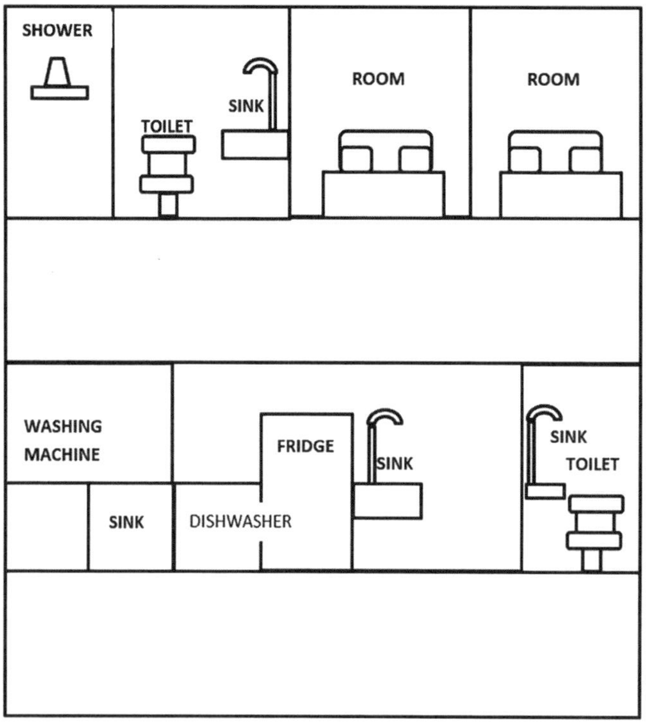

Bonus: Object of Your Choice

Choose an object that you would like to improve. It can be anything. Would you like your mattress to smell like gum? Would you like shoes to be as soft as cotton? Would you like the vegetables to have a layer of chocolate on top? Choose an object you would like to improve.

Draw the improvement and explain why you think your idea would improve it.

6. The Crisis Specialist

Time is very short in emergencies. You must decide the order of the steps to take to help in an emergency.

Example: Wicked Cat

You go in to your room holding a plastic glass of water. It seems that the neighbor's cat got in through the open window and is trying to catch your goldfish. It knocks the fishbowl off your desk and it shatters into dangerous pieces of glass. Your brother is crawling to play with the fish that landed on the floor. The cat also jumps to the floor to continue his mission to catch the fish.

In order, list the steps you would take to save your brother and the cat. Explain why.

First I would run to stop my brother from crawling. Then I would call for help and try to call the cat's attention away from the fish. When someone older arrives I will ask him to take the cat away from the broken fishbowl and place the fish in a glass of water.

Most important is the safety of my brother and me. The pieces of glass are dangerous. There could be small pieces near the fish. If I do not know the cat I will also stay away from it.

Challenge 1: Water Overflows

You are watching TV downstairs but realize it is time to take a bath. You take a towel and on your way to the bathroom you notice that there is a lot of water on the floor. The water is about to reach your mother's cell phone which is being charged on the floor, your father's laptop case, and the science project you've worked on for a month.

In order, list the steps you would take to save the cell phone, laptop case, and science project from the water. Explain why.

Challenge 2: Little Brother on Pool Slide

Your little brother is about to go on a zigzag slide that goes down to a deep pool. Your brother can't swim, and you do not know if you can help him out of the water without help. Your dad is far away from the pool, so he can't help you. You are at the pool, and there are some objects near you.

In order, list the steps you would take to help your brother get out of the pool. Explain why.

Challenge 3: Party Rescuer

Your mom just finished preparing for your sister's party. You enter your home with your dog and suddenly the leash slips away. The dog is heading toward a donkey piñata. Your brother is near the cupcakes, crying, looking toward the piñata. There is also a table with hot dogs and drinks for the children.

In order, list the steps you would take to save the piñata. Explain why.

Challenge 4: Delicious Costume

You and your sister are going to a costume party. You are dressed as a robot, and your sister has on a popcorn costume that she made herself. She glued a lot of popcorn to a shirt and a hat. A few minutes ago, a bird tried to eat some popcorn, but you scared it away. But now it is bringing some friends, and they seem determined to eat the popcorn.

In order, list the steps you would take to save your sister's costume. Explain why.

Challenge 5: Strong Wind

Your mother has a cold. She asks you to get the laundry that is drying on your patio. You go out with a basket and an umbrella, because the rain has already started to fall. The wind is blowing very hard, and it even flips your umbrella inside out. The sheets are losing the clothespins that hold them to the line. You also remember the very special flowers that your mother is caring for. They have recently bloomed.

In order, list the steps you would take to save the laundry and the flowers. Explain why.

Challenge 6: The Wedding

You are in a parking lot carrying a very fragile ice sculpture that has the wedding rings on it. You notice that an oily liquid is covering the ground you are walking on. It seems that a truck just spilled a lot of oil. You try to keep your balance, but you know you have to do something or the sculpture will end up broken on the ground and the rings could be lost. Your rented tuxedo is also in danger of getting difficult–to–remove stains.

In order, list the steps you would take to save the ice sculpture and your tuxedo. Explain why.

Challenge 7: Falling Purse

You and your mother are walking to the car in a parking lot. Your mother's purse starts to fall. The car keys, house keys, money, credit card, and cell phone are in danger of falling through the drain cover. It is also raining, and there are big puddles in the ground.

In order, list the steps you would take to save everything from falling in to the drain. Explain why.

Challenge 8: Splash

You are walking with your sister to the ballet show. You are carrying a cardboard tree for decorating the ballet and a jacket. You look over to the street and realize a car is passing over a puddle, and it is just about to splash your sister.

In order, list the steps you would take to save your sister. Explain why.

Challenge 9: Falling Box

You enter your brother's bedroom and see that a box is about to fall off the dresser. His pet turtle is in a tank just below it. You do not know if the box is so heavy that you could get injured if it fell on you as you try to remove the tank.

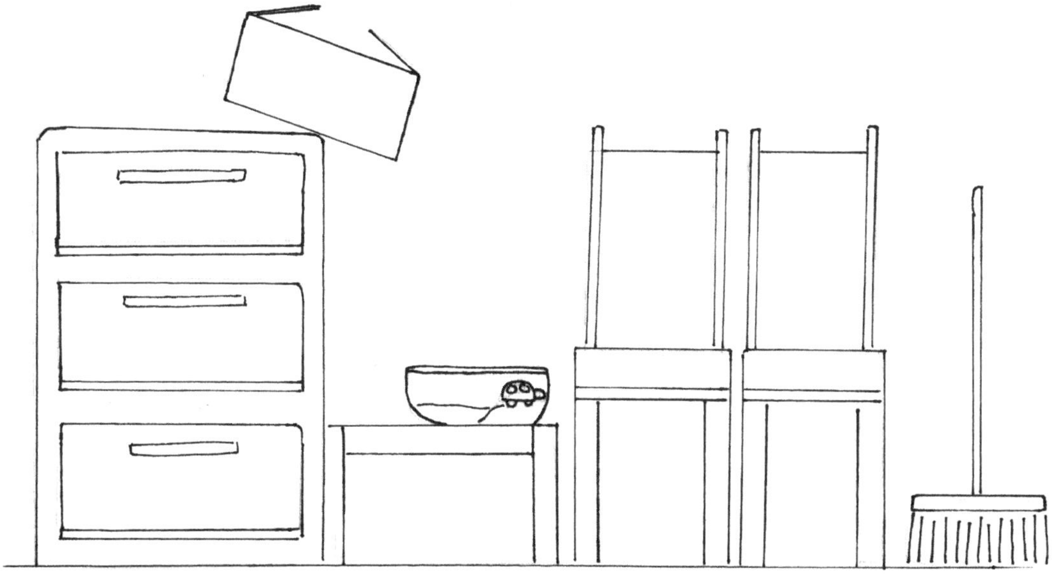

In order, list the steps you would take to save the turtle and not get hurt. Explain why.

City Challenge 1: The Bridges

Three bridges near you were damaged by a flood. Four messages have arrived for you below:

<u>From the city of Many People:</u> "The river rose a lot and destroyed Bridge 1. Our children go to classes at Town School and have not been able to get to the school."

<u>From Town School:</u> "We are teachers and have not been able to go back to our homes in Fruit Town because Bridge 2 fell. Please consider that two of us use a wheelchair."

<u>From Fruit Town:</u> "We have not sent our fruit trucks back to Many People City since the river took Bridge 3. The fruit will rot, and there will be a fruit shortage in the city. Please send us a bridge"

<u>From the city of Many People:</u> "We are the children. We are very happy we cannot go to school. We hope this is a long vacation! Do not send us a bridge."

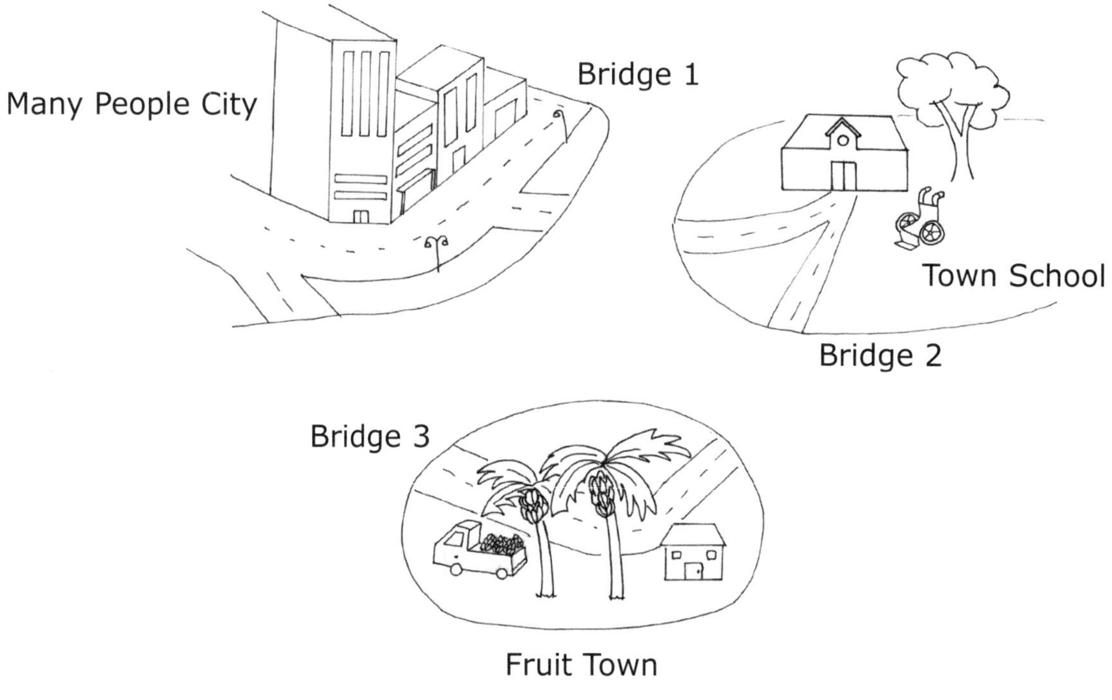

You have just two new bridges to use. Draw them where they are needed the most and write a letter explaining why.

____

____

____

City Challenge 2: Helicopter Help

Some people need your help while the bridges are being installed. You receive the following messages:

Message 1: "We are a group of 20 people on a tour at Town School. We cannot go back to the city because the bridge fell. We are staying at the school, but there is not enough food for everyone."

Message 2: "I am the manager of City Hospital. Our electric generator just failed. Our mechanic is on a tour of Town School. Please bring him here. It is urgent!"

Message 3: "My wife and I are in Fruit Town. We were near the bridge when it fell. My wife has a wounded leg, and I have to take her to the hospital for an X-ray."

Your friend: "Help me! I'm at the beach house near Fruit Town. I have an emergency! There are no lights and I cannot watch TV or play video games. Send the helicopter to rescue me!

Many People City

Town School

Fruit Town

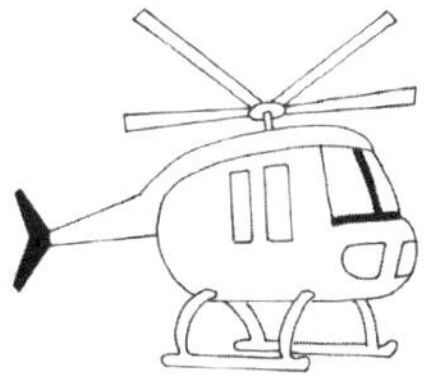

In order, list the instructions to the helicopter pilot. Explain why.

____

____

____

City Challenge 3: Assign the Money

The flood has caused some troubles and you have to give out money. You receive three requests, but you have money for just one of them.

Hospital Manager: "The river near the hospital overflowed to our parking lot. There are rocks and sticks all over. The river took pieces of the pavement, leaving some holes in it. You know how important the hospital is for the community"

Nursing Home Director: "The roof of the nursing home is damaged. There are large holes in one of the rooms, and water comes in when it rains."

School Principal: "A wall of the gym has cracks and the wind comes through. You know exercise and training is a very important part of our daily activities"

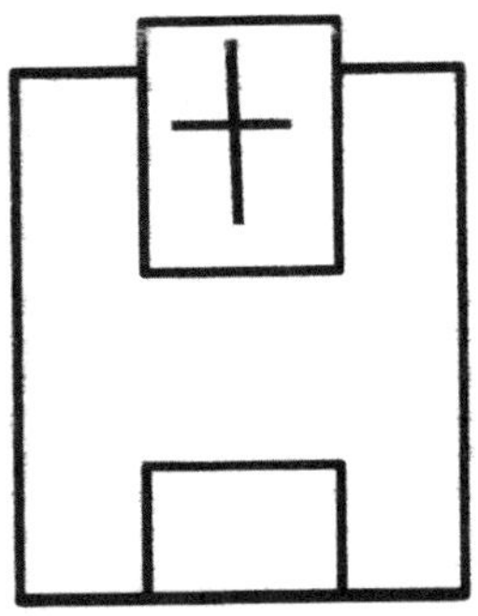

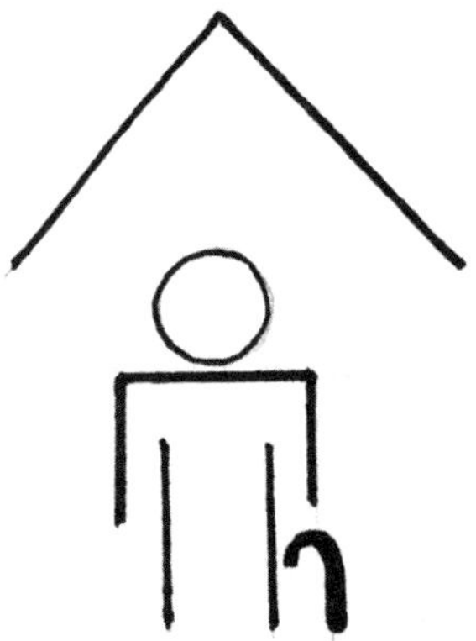

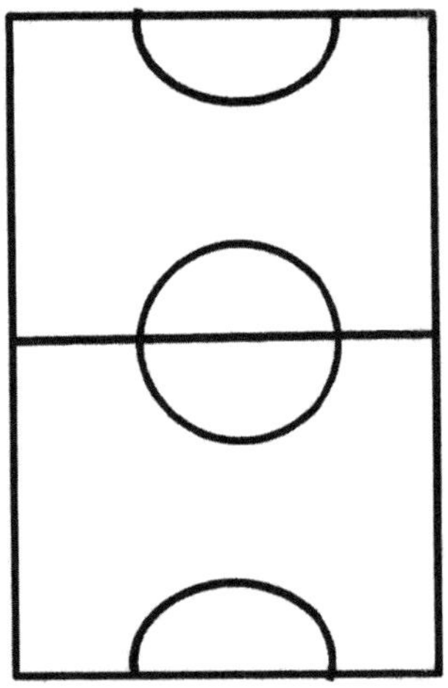

Who would get the money? Why?

City Challenge 4: The Airplane Space

Due to bad weather in the city of Many People, some flights were canceled. There are 6 free spaces in one of the planes and 11 people who need them. They are:

1. A family that is accompanying a grandmother to her knee surgery. They need 5 spaces for the grandmother, three adult daughters, and a grandson.
2. A mother with twins, three months old, who wants to go back home. They need 3 spaces.
3. An eight-year-old girl who was in a camp and travels alone to go back home. She needs 1 space.
4. Two elderly people who want to return home to the tropical climate. They feel very cold in the city of Many People. They need 2 spaces.

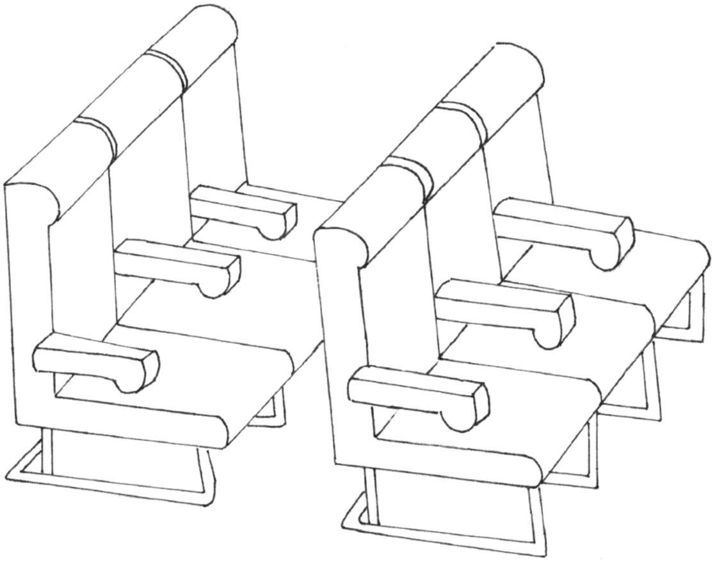

Who should get the seats? Why did you pick them?

____

____

____

____

____

City Challenge 5: Flooded Town

The water flooded some of the streets in the city. Some places are not able to be reached by car. The water can be removed with a water pump and tanker trucks, but it takes a lot of time. Look at the places and streets that are blocked by water.

What is the order the tanker trucks should use to remove the water?

____

____

Why did you choose that order?

____

____

____

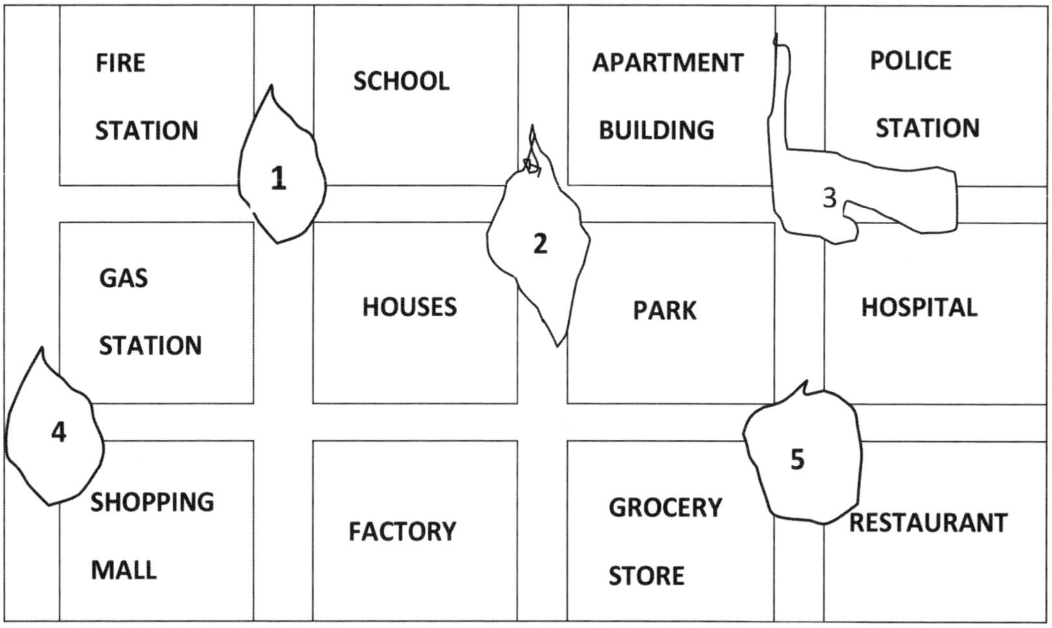

City Challenge 6: The City

One part of the city was damaged by the flood, and it will have to be rebuilt. The city planner sent you a draft of the new neighbourhoods. Looking at the plan, you realize that the school is very close to a factory. This factory makes smoke. Also it is good to be near the train, but the people prefer some distance from the noise to be able to sleep.

Fix the city plan.

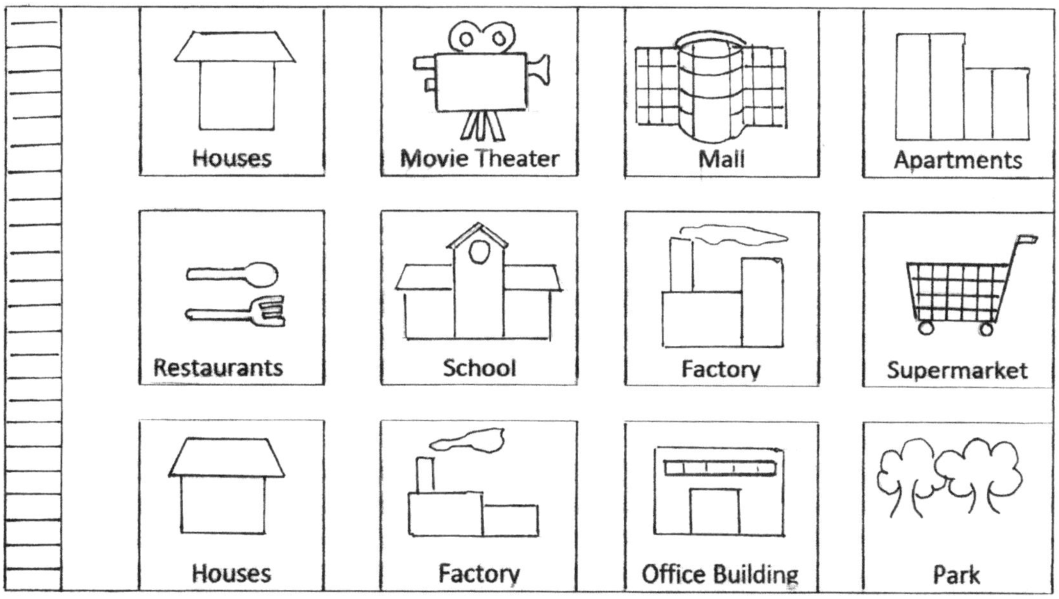

Your Plan for the City

7. The Best Tool

Choose the best tool to help in a situation.

Example: The Jewel

Your mother was cleaning the house and dropped a diamond earring in a glass vase. The vase is so valuable that it is attached to the table with glue.

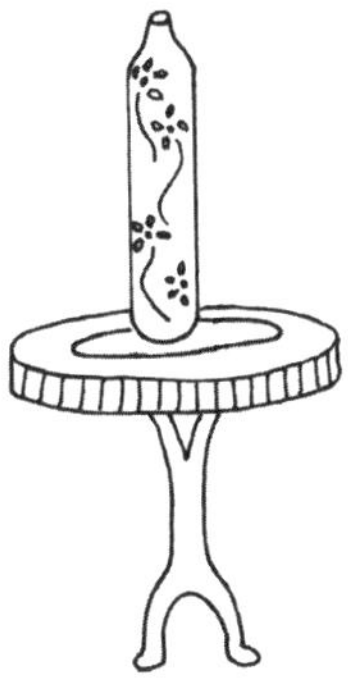

Tool Choices

Pliers **Chopsticks** **Tape** **Long Spoon** **Straws**

1. Which tool above would you choose to retrieve the earring? Explain why.

I would use the straws because they are soft and safer for the vase. I would make two long straws inserting the tip of the straw in a second straw. I would try to grab the earring with both long straws. Otherwise I would ask my mother to try to suction.

2. Could you add something to help you?

A piece of tape placed in the tip of the straw could help to grab the earring easier.

Challenge 1: Ants

Your ant colony has escaped your terrarium. There is a long line of ants going away from it. You see the queen among them.

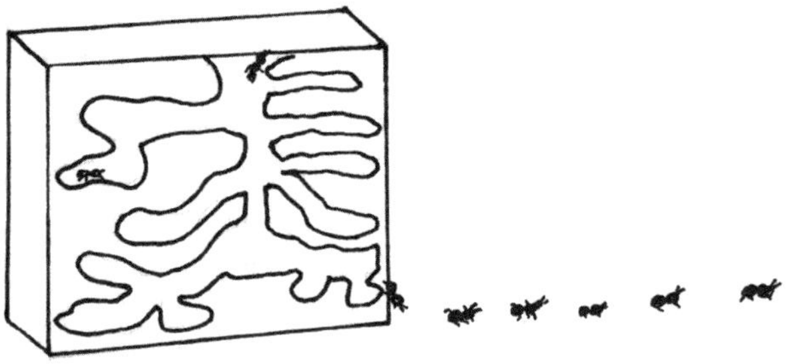

Tool Choices

Brush and Dust Pan

Tweezers

Hair Dryer (cool wind)

Brush

Hand Towel

1. Which tool above would you choose to guide the ants back to the terrarium?

2. Could you join them to make a new tool? How?

Challenge 2: Pick Up Leaves

Your grandmother asks you to pick up the leaves from her yard and take them to an organic recycling center a few blocks from her home. You look at the yard and think that it will take a lot of time to do it by hand.

Tool Choices

Old Sheets	Fan	Electrical Extension	Trash Picker	Metal DVD Holder	Bicycle
		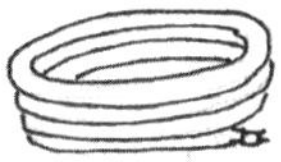	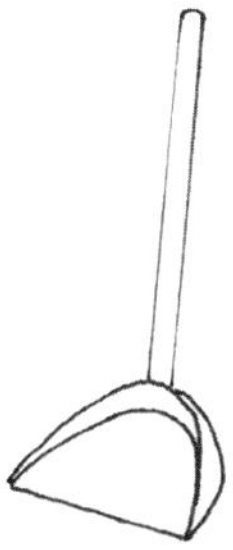	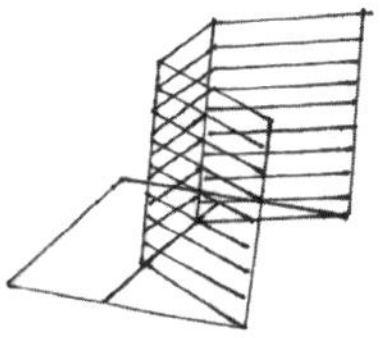	

1. Which tools above would you choose to help you take the leaves to the recycling center?

____

____

2. Could you join them to make a new tool? How?

____

____

Challenge 3: And Now... The Fruits!

You picked up the leaves so quickly from your grandmother's yard, that she asks you to help her pick the fruit from the trees, because she cannot reach that high and does not have a ladder. She knows you'll come up with some way to do it.

Tool Choices

Golf Club | **Plastic Bottle** | **Fish Hook** | **Knife With Saw Blade** | **Broom** | **Tape**

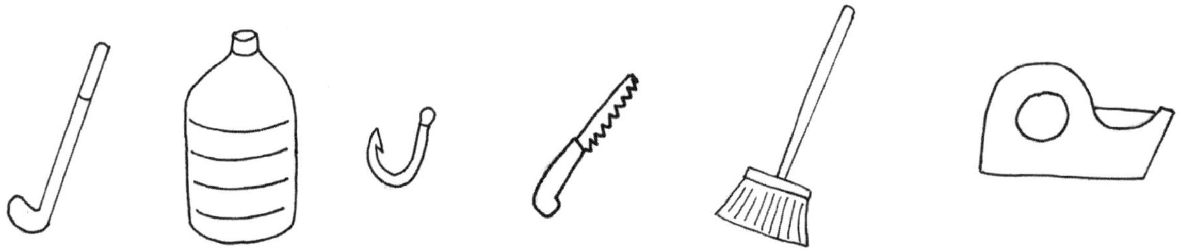

1. Which tools above would you choose to help you pick the apples?

____

____

2. Could you join them to make a new tool? How?

____

____

Challenge 4: Change of Rope

Ten years ago you made a bird feeder. Every week you loosen the end of the rope hooked on the trunk of the tree and the feeder comes down. You fill it with seeds and pull the rope to raise it up. The rope is about to break and you need to change it. The tree has grown a lot since you made the feeder. You want to do it alone, but your parents will not let you climb a ladder that high. You will have to think of some way to achieve it from the ground. Remember to insert the rope through the hole in the branch to keep the feeder from moving when it is windy.

Tool Choices

Tape	Fishing Rod	Dart	Safety Pin	Rope

1. Which tools above would you choose to help you replace the rope?

____

____

2. Could you join them to make a new tool? How?

____

____

Challenge 5: Helping the Bird

A baby bird has fallen from a tree. You must think of a way to return it to the nest. The nest is at a height that can be reached with a stool. You have to decide the best way to transfer the bird back to the nest.

Tool Choices

Plastic Plate	Plastic Bowl	Basketball Net	Towel	Baseball Glove

1. Which tools above would you choose to help you transfer the bird to the nest?

____

____

2. Could you join them to make a new tool? How?

____

____

Challenge 6: The Fish Tank

Your grandmother has a fish tank. There are very big fish and little baby fish. The babies are usually near their mother. Your grandmother thinks is better to move the babies to a different tank, but she has not being able to do it. They are very fast, and the tank is so big it is very difficult to catch one.

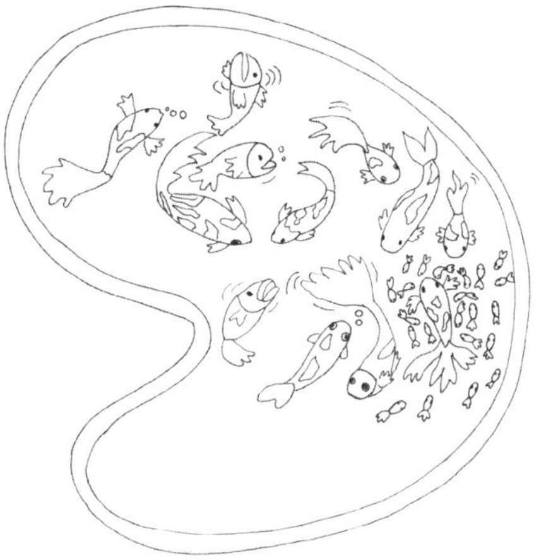

Tool Choices

Box

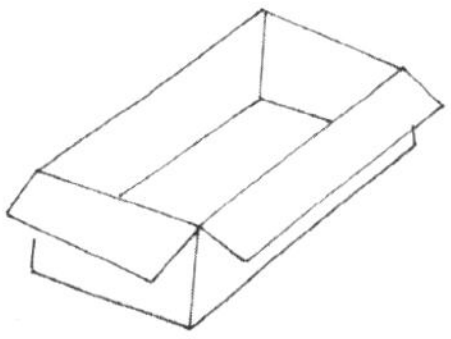

Fish Tank Net

Plastic Bag

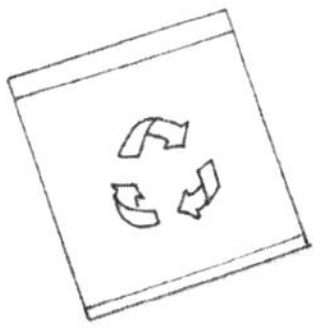

Garbage Can

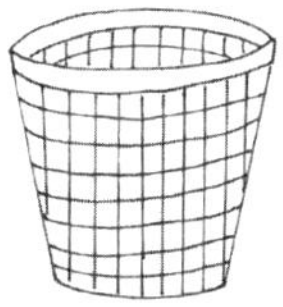

Toy Tunnel

1. Which tools above would you choose?

____

____

2. Could you join them to make a new tool? How?

____

____

Challenge 7: Brother Alarm

Your brother has been trying to startle you. If you can think of some alarm system that will let you know when he has opened the door, he will not be able to scare you.

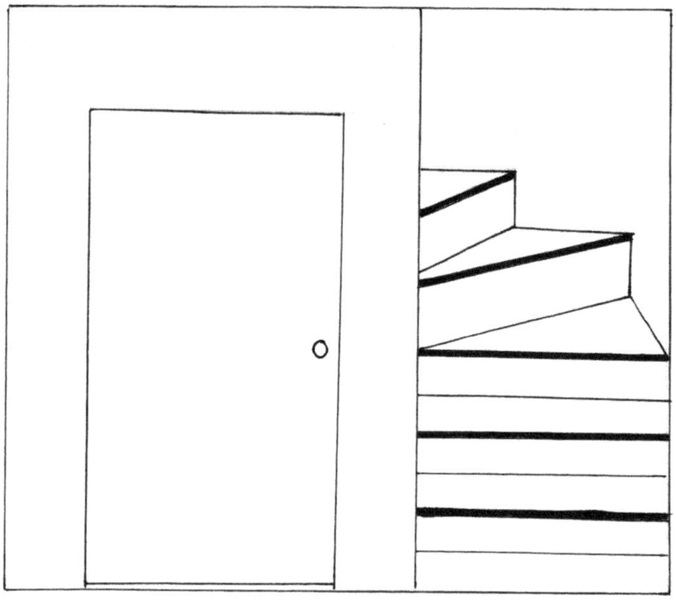

Tool Choices

Drum

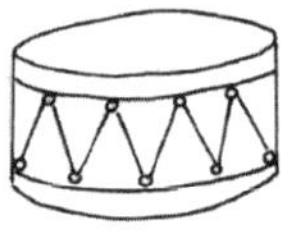

Bottle

Bell

Glass

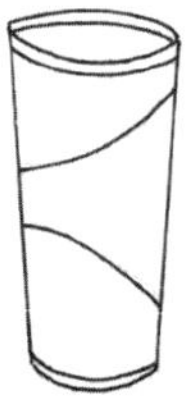

Cymbals

1. Which ones would you choose to prevent your brother from scaring you?

____

____

2. Could you join them to make a new tool? How?

____

____

Challenge 8: Sharing Toys

Matt and Nico live in separate apartments facing each other, but Nico's apartment is one story up. They can see each other from their bedroom windows. They want to share their toy cars using the windows. They have found some items that they think will work to make their "sharing bridge." The biggest challenge they think they have is that Nico's room is one story up. In order to build the bridge, they can meet and give each other the items they each need.

Tool Choices

Clothes Hanger | **Small Bag** | **Cotton Balls** | **Rope** | **Stick (it gets halfway)** | **Helium Balloons** | **Spring**

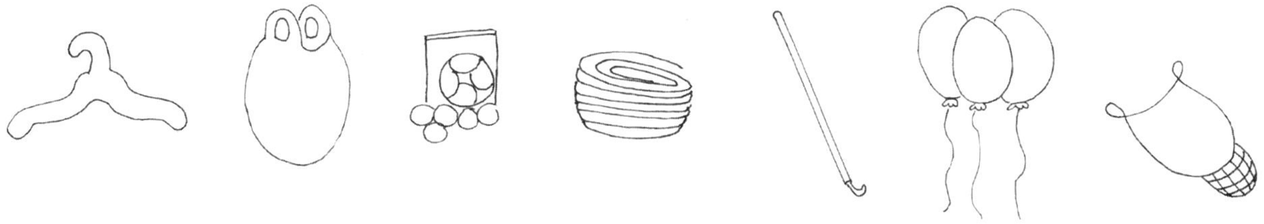

1. Which tools above would you choose to build the bridge?

____

____

2. Could you join them to make a new tool? How?

____

____

Challenge 9: Hot Sand

You are swimming and the strong waves take your flip flops out to sea. You have to get out of the water and pick up the things you left on the sand. There are many stones on the beach and the sand is boiling.

Using the objects you see in the picture, how would you get up the beach?

Challenge 10: Deep Hole

A dog dug a large hole in the school yard and went to sleep in it. You send him home, but now you need to fill the hole quickly, so the little kids are not in danger of falling in. The worst thing is that it rained and the dirt was washed away from the hole. At the back of the school yard, there is a storage shed where you can see the following: old deflated footballs, a boot, a shirt and trousers, party hats, glasses, and party plates.

Using the objects you see in the picture, how would you fill in the hole?

Challenge 11: Crossing the River

A river overflowed its banks and you and your cat are standing on a plastic table out of the water. There is a larger plastic table, an igloo ice chest, and a plastic chair nearby. On the other side of the river there is a dry, safe area where you can expect to be rescued. The river is barely moving. If you get down from the table, the water will probably reach your waistline. You could swim it without problem, but your cat is terrified of the water, and the water is so cold that you would hate to get wet.

Using the objects you see in the picture, how would you and your cat cross the river?

Challenge 12: Measuring the Couches

Your mother wants to surprise your grandmother. She wants to buy her two new couches, exactly the same sizes she already has. She asks you to measure the couches while she distracts your grandmother, but she forgot to bring a measuring tape. You need to measure the couches height and length while you are alone in the room.

Using the objects you see in the picture, how would you measure the couches?

Challenge 13: Naughty Dog

You are about to make cookies. You left the flour on the table when you went in to the family room. When you come back to the kitchen you find out your big dog, Jack, made a mess. Since your mother already cleaned the house, you cannot let Jack walk around covered in flour. You have to take him to the shower without spreading more flour, but he is too big to carry in your arms.

Using the objects you see in the picture, how would you get your dog to the shower?

____

____

____

____

____

____

____

Challenge 14: School Shoes

You are on your way home from school. There is a big mud puddle in your way. You are wearing your school shoes. You do not want to get them dirty, because if you wash them they will not be dry for the next day.

Using the objects you see in the picture, how would you get home without getting your shoes wet?

Challenge 15: Teacher's Pen

You were playing with your teacher's pen and it ended up going through the open window and falling to the first floor roof. There is a high cliff on that side of the building. If the pen falls off the roof, it will be lost. Your arm does not stretch far enough to reach the pen using the open window.

Using the objects you see in the picture, how would you get the pen?

8. The Enigma*

Use your imagination to discover the enigmas.

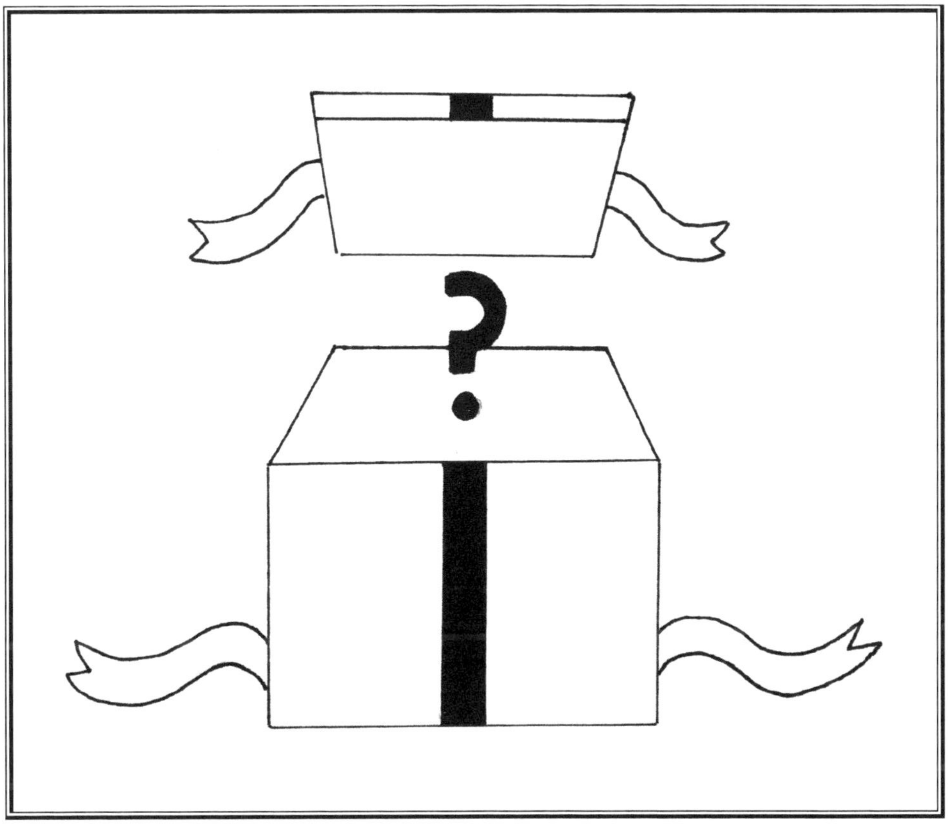

*A person or thing that is mysterious, puzzling, or difficult to understand.

Example

1. What do you think this figure is? Write all the ideas that come to mind below the figure.

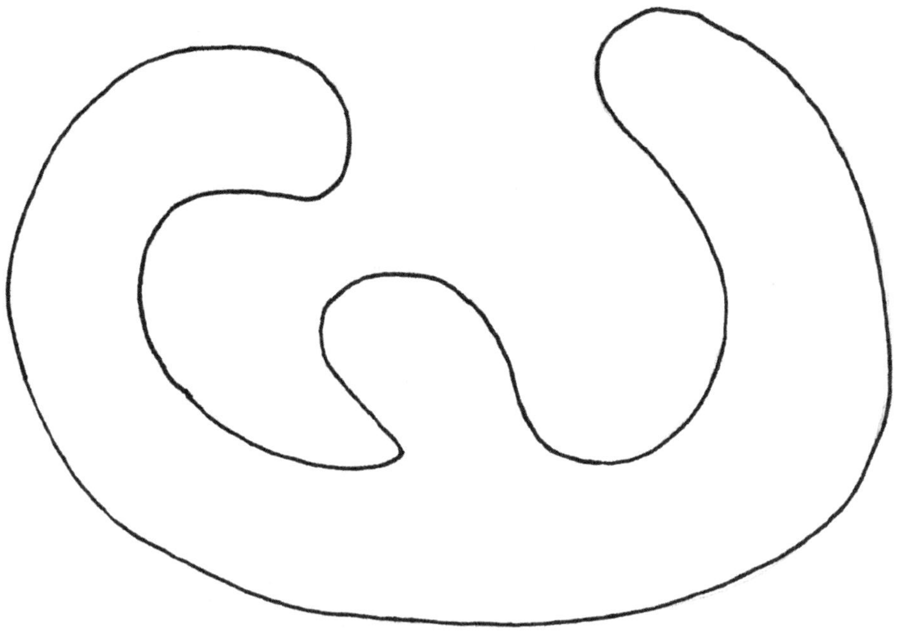

Here are some ideas: a crab, a 3 or an E, a bull's nose, hugging a pillow, or a trident

2. Choose one of the ideas above and complete the drawing. You can flip the figure, or make it bigger or smaller. The bull's nose was used in the example.

Enigma 1

1. What do you think this figure is? Write all the ideas that come to mind below the figure.

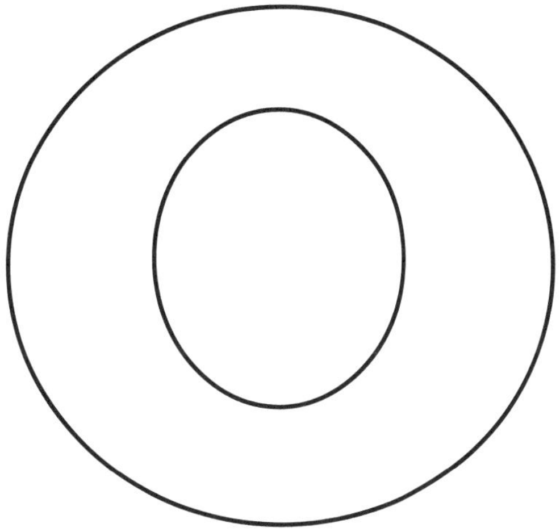

2. Complete the drawing choosing one of your ideas. You can flip the figure, or make it bigger or smaller.

Enigma 2

1. What do you think this figure is? Write all the ideas that come to mind below the figure.

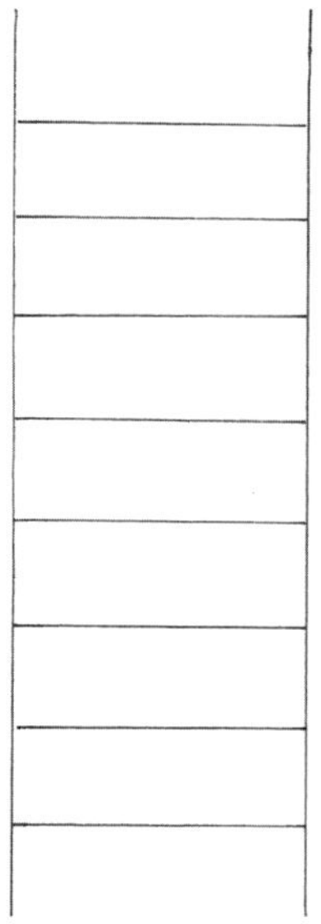

2. Complete the drawing choosing one of your ideas. You can flip the figure, or make it bigger or smaller.

Enigma 3

1. What do you think this figure is? Write all the ideas that come to mind below the figure.

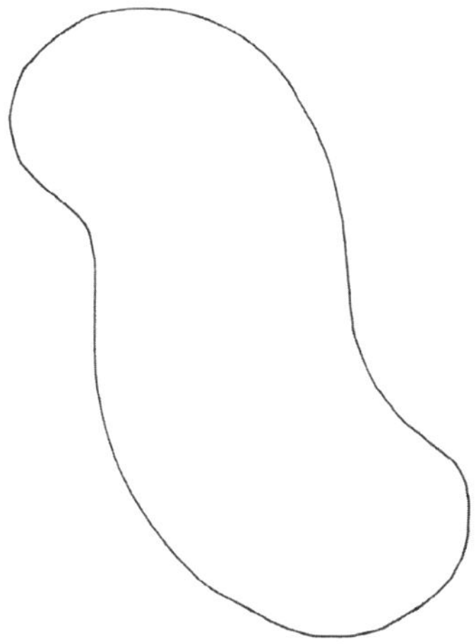

2. Complete the drawing choosing one of your ideas. You can flip the figure, or make it bigger or smaller.

Enigma 4

1. What do you think this figure is? Write all the ideas that come to mind below the figure.

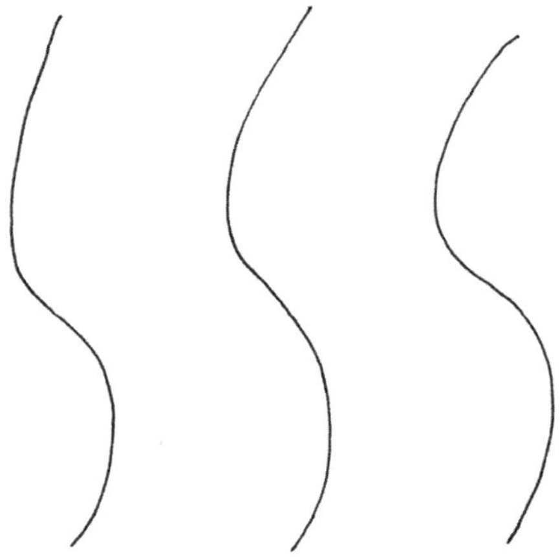

2. Complete the drawing choosing one of your ideas. You can flip the figure, or make it bigger or smaller.

Enigma 5

1. What do you think this figure is? Write all the ideas that come to mind below the figure.

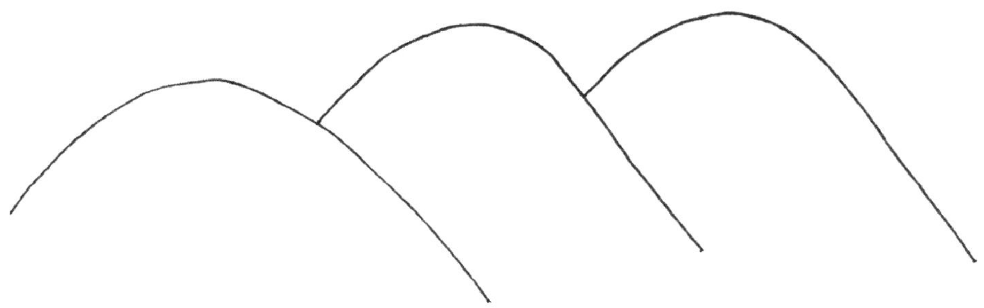

2. Complete the drawing choosing one of your ideas. You can flip the figure, or make it bigger or smaller.

Enigma 6

1. What do you think this figure is? Write all the ideas that come to mind below the figure.

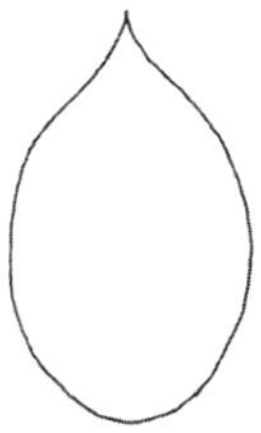

2. Complete the drawing choosing one of your ideas. You can flip the figure, or make it bigger or smaller.

Enigma 7

1. What do you think this figure is? Write all the ideas that come to mind below the figure.

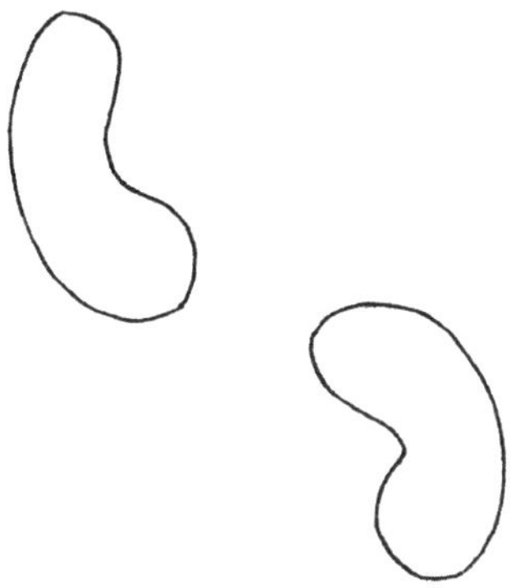

2. Complete the drawing choosing one of your ideas. You can flip the figure, or make it bigger or smaller.

Enigma 8

Mark each figure you find below with a different color.

Enigma 9

You and your friend made up a game. You take turns hiding candies from each other. To find the candies, you have to find a clue and solve it. The clue could be a puzzle map, crossword, number, word, or combination of a number and a word. It may lead to another clue.

Your friend gives you this clue, "It starts with the lady with the hat. Each figure is looking or pointing at the next clue. The last figure is looking at ? ___________ (the last word is the clue). If you are in doubt, take a closer look and find out."

1. Point to or number the clues in order.

2. Write the word: ___________________________

Enigma 10

Your friend tells you the next clue is the highest number in the ball dispenser.

What do the numbers you can see have in common? What is the highest number that you cannot see?

Write the number: ______________________________

Enigma 11

Now your friend gives you the drawings below.

Enter the code: ______________________________

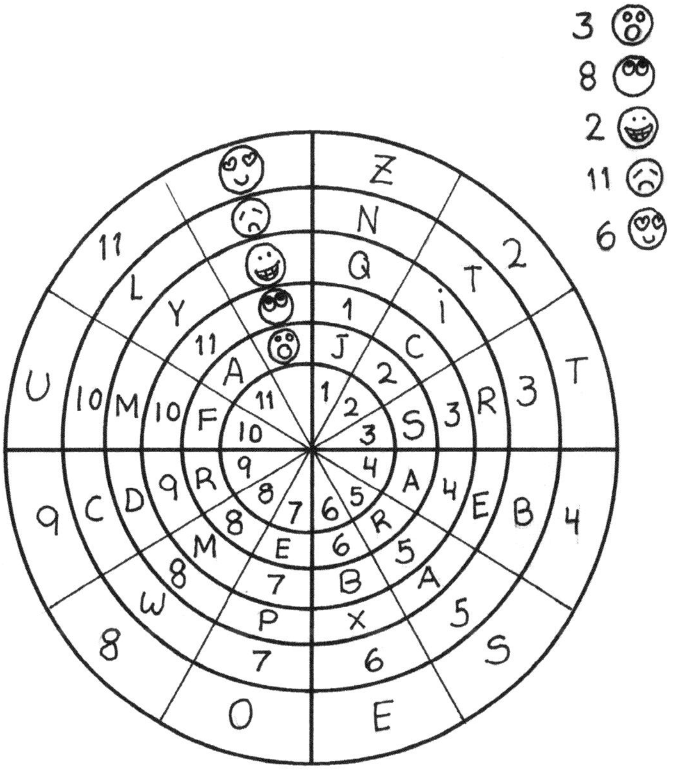

Enigma 12

To find the next code, cut out the large rectangle on the next page and roll it over a #2 pencil until the letters reveal the code. (Or cut a rectangle ½″ wide and 8½″ long and draw the letters.)

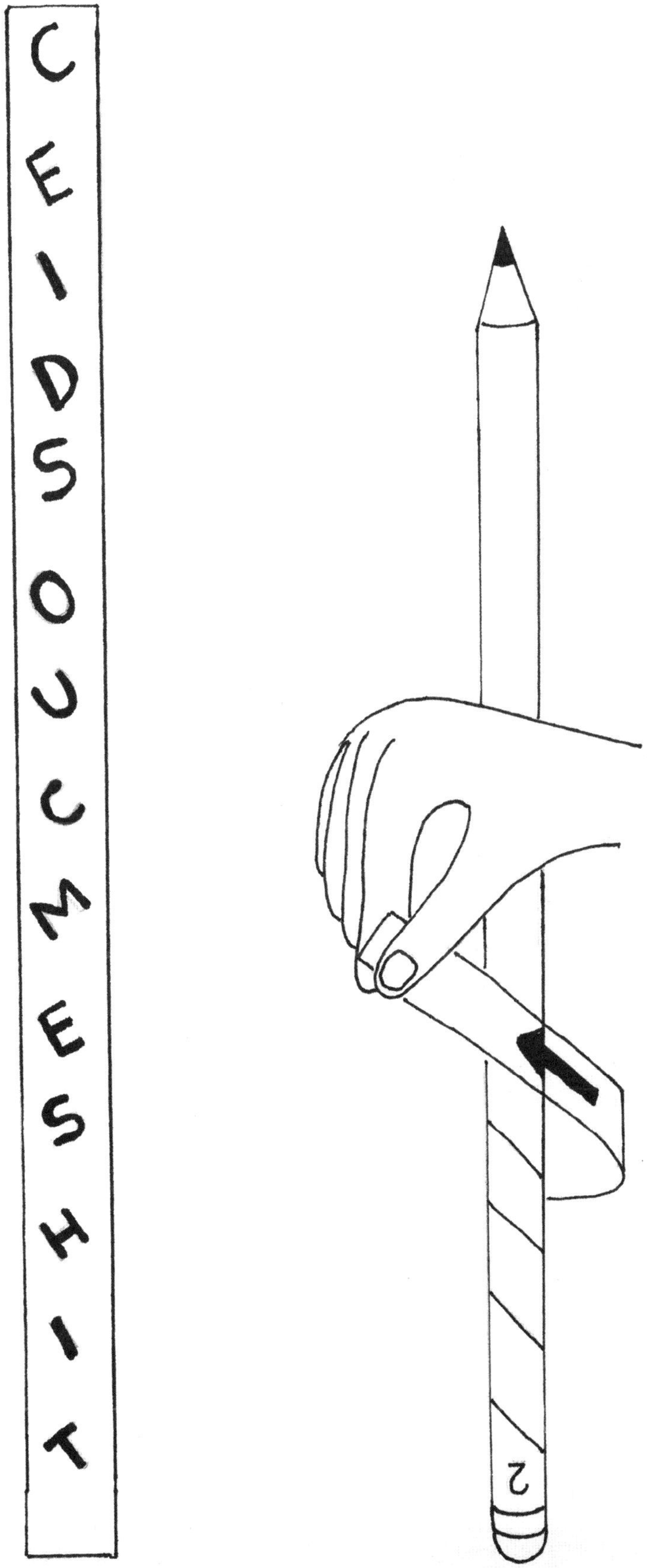
C
E
I
D
S
O
U
C
M
E
S
H
I
T

Enigma 13

Now your friend gives you the drawings below. This is a puzzle. Only four stick men have the necessary tools to fit one into the other. The tool of the right hand must be able to join with the left of the following one. The word is formed with the letters of the stick men' hats.

What is the word? ______________________________

Enigma 14

Your friend tells you that each figure below has four pieces inside. There is one correct order to separate the pieces. You have to remove them one at a time. Some pieces are interlocked, making it necessary to move one before moving the other. The code is the four numbers in the order they have to be removed to separate the pieces.

Enter the 4-number code: ______________________________

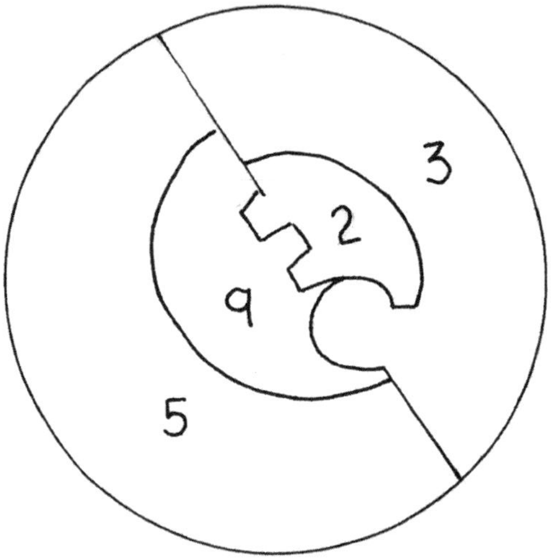

Enigma 15

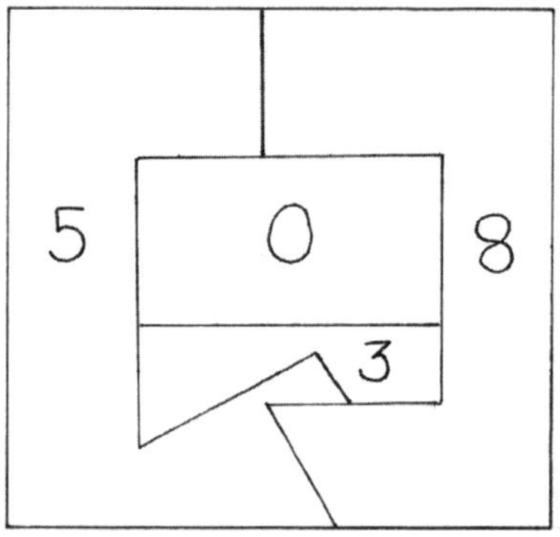

Enter the 4-number code: ______________________________

Enigma 16

Here is your message: Stick man is the clue to the four-letter word you are looking for.

Enter the 4-letter word: ______________________________

Enigma 17

Your friend gives you the drawing below and tells you: The next code is two words. Hint: Look for it in a mirror.

Enter the two-word code: ______________________________

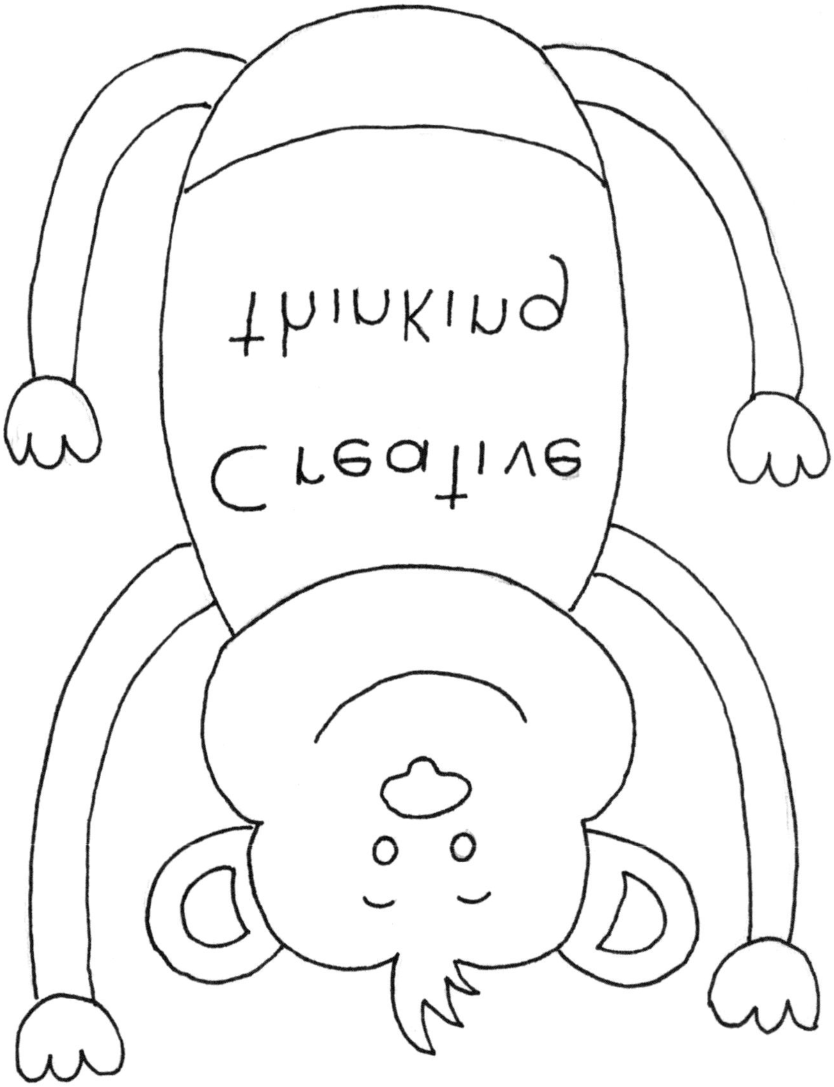

9. The Mind Ride

Shut your eyes and imagine you are a character in a story.

Ask someone to read the following story while you shut your eyes and go for a mind ride.

Example: Ride 1

You are walking through a forest. You hear what sounds like the flapping of small wings approaching, and then two fairies fly next to your head. You keep walking and suddenly you hear a whisper "Watch out!" You stop and look down at a goblin. He is mad because you were about to step on his house. You move aside and continue walking. You feel a gentle touch in your head. You look up and discover that a tree branch is touching it. "Your hair feels very soft," he tells you, "softer than my leaves." The sound is coming out of a mouth in the middle of the trunk of the tree. Just above it you see brilliantly shinning eyes looking at you. You are too surprised to reply. Suddenly you feel the vibration of heavy steps on the ground. First you think that the tree might be lifting his roots. But then you hear heavy footsteps coming behind the tree. "I cannot look behind my back," the tree tells you. "Please go and see what it is and tell me." The sound is louder now and you feel the ground vibrate even stronger. You look and see....

Tell the tree what you saw.

Something is emerging from the ground. It is like a small lump of moving, living earth. It appears from the grass and grows taller than the trees. Then it disappears and appears again in a different place nearby. It seems to be looking for someone, especially because of that alarm sound that is coming from it. Suddenly a mini lump appears laughing. The bigger lump appears beside the small one, and they disappear together.

Ask someone to read the following story while you shut your eyes and go for a mind ride.

Ride 2

You have two baseballs. You are going to meet your friend in the park. He will bring the bat. You go outside of your house and come to a high fence. You think it will be quicker to climb over the fence to get to the park. You leave one ball on the ground and put the other in your right pants pocket so you can climb over the fence. You place your feet one on top of the other, and your hands help you balance as you go up step-by-step. When you feel that you are well balanced, you hurry and climb even faster. You reach the top of the fence and take a big jump to the ground on the other side. You continue walking and come to a small apple tree that you climb by putting a foot on the trunk and reaching a branch with your hand to pull you up. Then you sit on a large branch to see where the apples are and try to reach some. You stretch your arm to grab one and immediately take a bite. It is sweet and refreshing. You reach for another to take it to your friend and put it in your left pants pocket. Now you slide to the lowest part of the branch and jump from the tree. You are not far away from the park. You come to a puddle of water, put your feet in it, and jump up and down many times to empty the water from the puddle. Then you hear a voice calling your name. It's your friend. You run to meet him and he asks if you remembered to bring the balls. You say yes and touch the right pants pocket and feel nothing. You check the left pocket and take out an apple.

Tell your friend where you think you might have lost the baseballs so you can go get them.

Ask someone to read the following story while you shut your eyes and go for a mind ride.

Ride 3

You're riding your bike. You pedal slowly because you are climbing a mountain. There are pine trees by the side of the road. The wind is very cold and your arms feel very cold. You ride your bike to the side of the road to get your jacket out of your backpack. You lean the bicycle on one of the pine trees and take off your backpack. You open it to grab your jacket, but you have to move everything because it seems to be at the bottom. You find a notepad, sandwich, water, and a folding umbrella. You pull out your jacket and put it on.

Then you see some pine cones on the ground that you can use to make crafts at home. You pick them up, but there are so few that you decide to climb the tree to pick a few more. Before you climb up you hear some dry leaves crunching. You think it is footsteps because the crunching is getting louder. You do not see anyone. Suddenly you see the back of an animal. Now you see a pair of wild boars. You know they can be very aggressive. Who knows if you could face one, but two? You think quickly what to do—what you have at hand and what you carry in the backpack. You have seconds to climb the tree or try to get on the bike.

What would you do?

___

___

___

___

___

___

___

___

___

___

Ask someone to read the following story while you shut your eyes and go for a mind ride.

Ride 4

You are a sailor who explores of oceans. But you are also an ingenious inventor. You have added all kinds of devices to your ship to be able to dive to the depths of the sea. You especially like it when your radar warns you about a new abyss that you have not yet explored.

You start to descend in to the water and see how the blue color changes in intensity as you move away from the surface. You reach a depth where everything looks absolutely black, not even a little hint of blue or dark gray. You turn off the lights and the propeller of your ship to see and listen but there is nothing, absolutely nothing. It is like you have unplugged your senses. At the same time, your sense of intuition is activated. And your intuition tells you that you are being observed or perhaps "felt" by something that does not see you either. You feel IT is near you, behind you. You decide to gently turn the ship. You do not turn on the lights yet, because you do not want to scare your observer. At first you do not distinguish anything, but then you discover a silhouette. An area that is darker than its surroundings. You turn on the lights and you see IT. It is the most amazing underwater creature you have ever seen.

Describe IT.

____

____

____

____

____

____

____

____

____

Ask someone to read the following story while you shut your eyes and go for a mind ride.

Ride 5

You are on a school field trip to a scientist's lab. Doctor Crazyeyes is introduced to you. Not only does the name sound weird, but the man in front of you looks strange. He has what seems to be a pot on his head and a long metal spoon in his hand. He tells you he is doing experiments about sound waves, and he wants to feel and hear vibrations in his head. He asks each of you to come close and hit the pot with the spoon to feel your transmissions. He probably ended up feeling a little dizzy, because he says he's going to sit down for a while. He asks you to look around his lab while he recovers. Each of your classmates goes separate ways. You observe a line of balloons. Different gloves squeeze each balloon, pumping out the gas and making them whistle. The balloons are reinflated and then squeezed again. You keep moving and are in front of a door with the label "Extreme Experiment." It must be the best experiment, or the most dangerous. Who knows? The temptation is very strong. You open the door and enter the room.

Stay with your eyes closed and think about what is inside that door.

Professor Crazyeyes takes you out of the room as soon as he returns and did not allow anyone else to see the Extreme Experiment. Now we are back at the school bus, and your classmates ask you about the Extreme Experiment.

Tell your friends what you saw.

Ask someone to read the following story while you shut your eyes and go for a mind ride.

Ride 6

Your friends ask you to join them for the ultimate 3-D experience. They did not tell you exactly what it is about, just that it is spectacular, and that you have to try it. They want it to be a surprise.

At the 3-D Experience store, each of you is given a tag with your name on it. All of you stick them on your shirts.

Two of your friends enter first and you go right behind them.

As soon as you enter, you discover the most astonishing nature landscape you have ever seen. You do not know where to start looking. It is like a giant zoo with a lot of habitats very close together. The Arctic is to your right, the woods are in front of you, and the sea is to your left.

Suddenly one of your friends transforms in to a dolphin. You know it is your friend, because he still has the name tag near his head. He smiles at you and laughs like a dolphin. Water bubbles surround him and moves him very fast to the sea section.

Another friend transforms in to an eagle. He spreads his wings and waves you good-bye as he rises to the mountains.

A third friend arrives at your side. You ask him how to transform. He says. "You just have to choose an animal. Then start thinking you are becoming it. Try to imagine how your skin feels and what sounds you will make. Then imagine yourself moving, flying, running, or swimming. As soon as you reach an intense and vivid image of you being that animal, you will become it. Then you will be taken to its habitat.

Two seconds later your friend becomes a polar bear. It shows you its big paws and gives you a high-five before leaving for the Arctic.

Now it is your turn.

You think of the animal you want to become. Start picturing how it looks... how it smells... how it sounds. Take your time.

You now have become that animal and are being taken to its habitat.

Look at everything around you. Look for other animals that live there. Look at your surroundings.

Now open your eyes and describe the animal you became. Explain how you felt being the animal and what you saw.

Ask someone to read the following story while you shut your eyes and go for a mind ride.

Ride 7

You have been selected as the first person to travel through time. You mission is to travel a hundred years in the future to explore the new inventions that are available.

You receive requests from a lot of scientists, doctors, cell phone companies, and car factories. They all want you to take a look at the inventions in their fields. They are interested about the latest medical cures, how are people of the future are producing food, how are they traveling, and how are they dealing with contamination.

The head of the mission tells you there is a time limit to be in the future. You have been chosen because you had the highest score on the Critical Thinking Test. You enter the traveling chamber wondering if tomorrow's problems will be the same as today's. You try to boost your confidence to get ready. You tell yourself, "I am smart. I will know what to look for."

Suddenly you are going at a very high speed; the chamber is getting very warm while the molecules are getting smaller. You do not open your eyes, because you do not want to get dizzy, but a lot of beams of colors get through your closed eyes. Then the chamber gets very cold and in an instant it stops. You hear the sound of the door opening. You are now in the future. You start walking around.

1. Tell what you see.

____

____

____

____

____

____

____

____

2. Which invention do you think is the most important in the future?

3. Which invention from the future would like to exist now to make your life easier or funnier?

Ask someone to read the following story while you shut your eyes and go for a mind ride.

Ride 8

Your last mission to the future was very successful. Scientists will not be able to send you to the future again for a few years because of all the energy that is needed. The subatomic charger has just enough energy to send you ten years back in the past. You have some important decisions to make.

1. Which invention that was made in the last ten years would you take to the people in the past? (You can search the Internet to find out about the inventions.)

____

____

____

When you arrive ten years in the past you would have just a half hour before the chamber has to take you back to your present time.

2. Who would you contact to give the information about the invention you brought with you?

____

____

____

3. What other information would you like to deliver to someone ten years in the past?

____

____

____

Ask someone to read the following story while you shut your eyes and go for a mind ride.

Ride 9

You've been in space for a few months. Your mission is to find life on planets other than Earth. You are visiting Jupiter's moons. However, you have not managed to find a single being yet. There isn't any trace at all. Today, you have decided to land on a moon that you have never been to. You put on your spacesuit and go down with your microscope, hoping to find even the tiniest of creatures. Suddenly you hear a noise, a sound of water moving smoothly, similar to a washing machine. You see what looks like a simple rock falling from the sky, possibly a meteor. You would not have even noticed it except for the sound of the water. It lands softly so it might not be a meteor.

You approach with great anxiety and start taking pictures. The stone is motionless. Suddenly you hear a whoosh and the stone opens up in to two halves. Inside is an alien so small it would easily fit on your hand. You do not know how much of what you see is the alien and how much is its spacesuit. As you are looking at the alien, it is looking back at you. You can see through its mask that it is smiling, as happy to see you as you are to see it.

1. Draw the alien.

The alien begins to talk to you in a shrill voice. It spends several seconds screaming excitedly until you start to talk back. You want it to realize what it probably already knew but forgot that you speak a totally different language. It closes its mouth and takes out a device from his ship. It is a projector that illuminates the space between you. Soon it shows you a short movie about its planet. It seems that the alien came better prepared than you.

Then you remember to communicate your discovery to NASA.

2. Write the message to NASA letting them know about the alien. Tell them everything you saw in the movie.

____

____

____

The alien is waiting for you to show it something. Tell it about Earth through pictures.

3. Search the Internet for pictures that show what you want him to know about planet Earth. Paste them on the next page.

Why did you choose these pictures?

Print and paste your pictures.

4. The alien drew the picture below and gave it to you. What do you think it means?

____

____

____

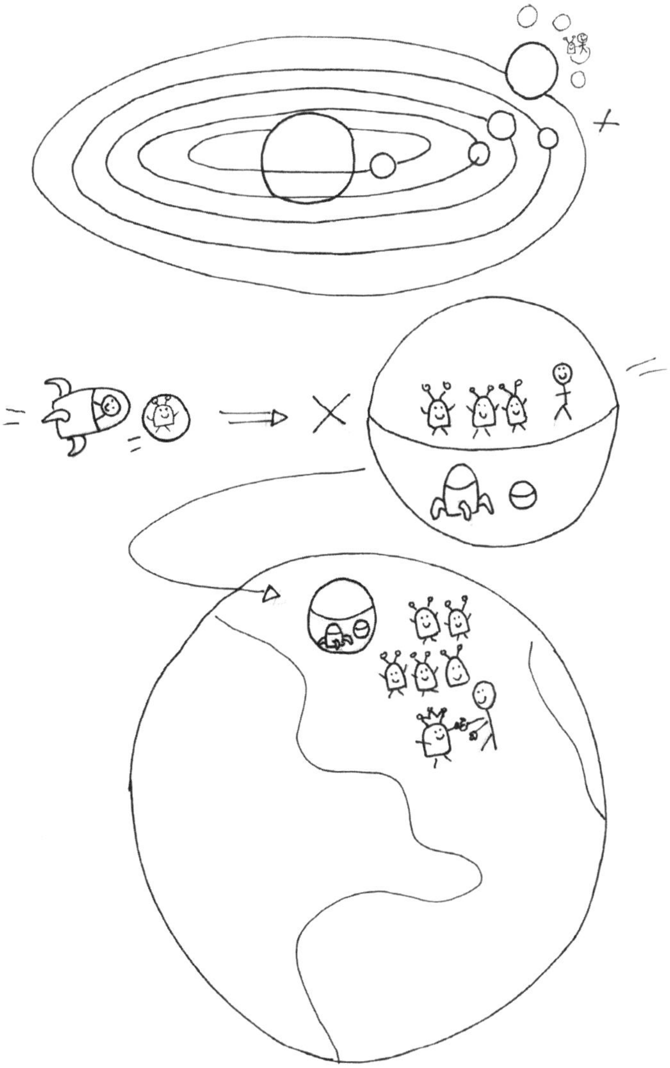

Super Challenge

10. 2-D and 3-D Figures and Shading

Have fun playing with 2-D and 3-D figures.

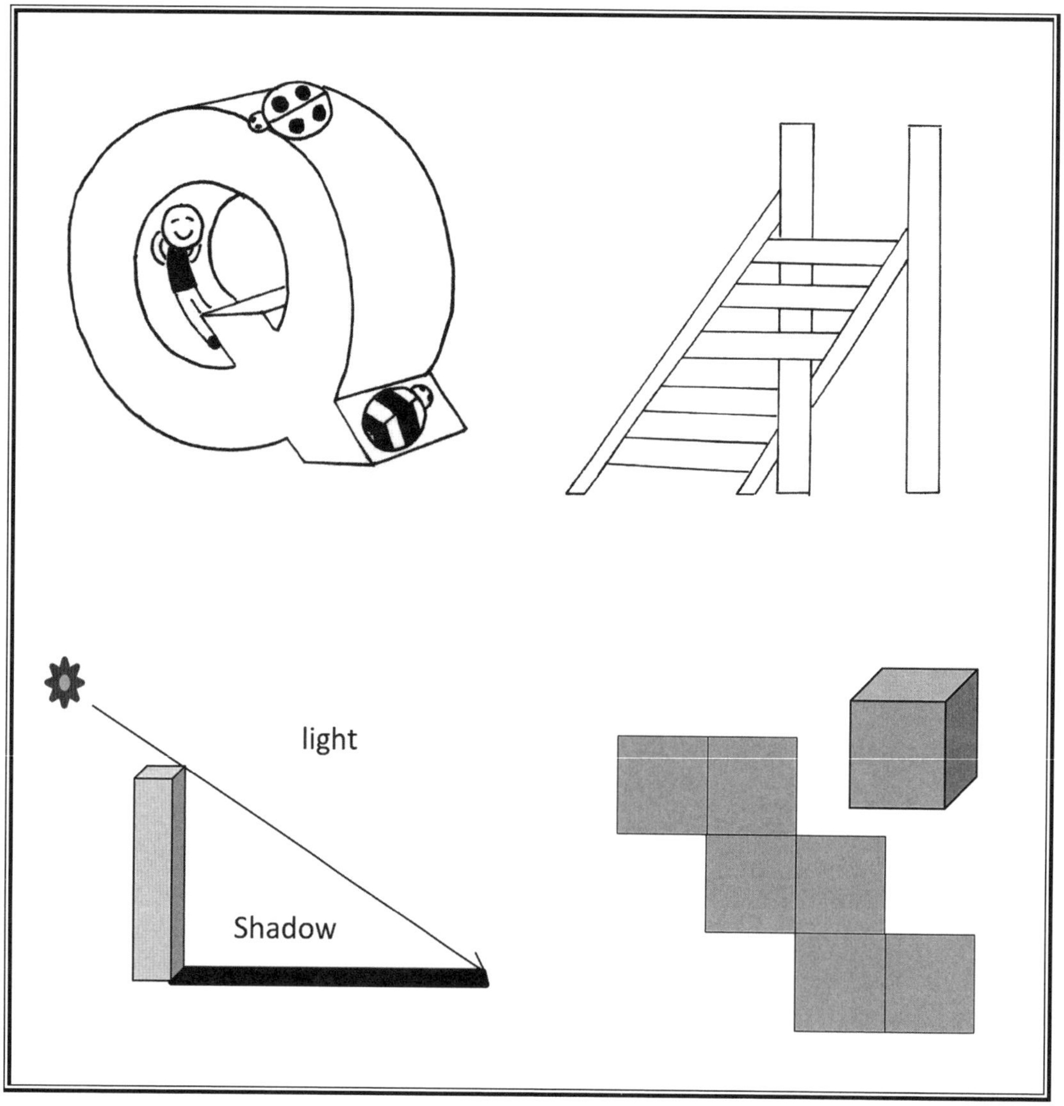

2-D and 3-D Shapes

2-D shapes have 2 dimensions.

The top of the train (figure 1) shows 2 dimensions: width and depth.

The front of the train (figure 2) shows 2 dimensions: height and depth.

3-D shapes have 3 dimensions.

Figure 3 shows three dimensions: height, width, and depth.

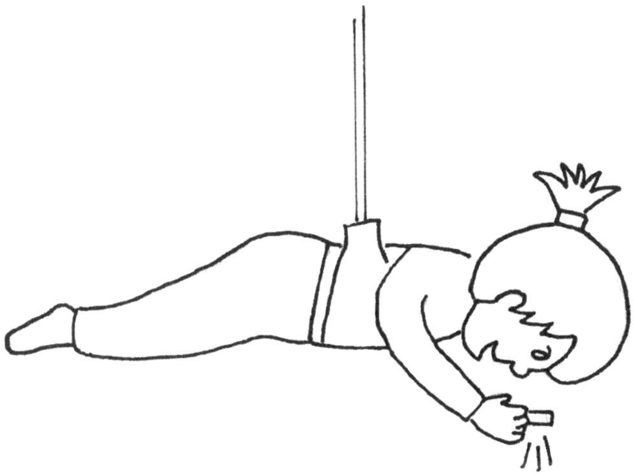

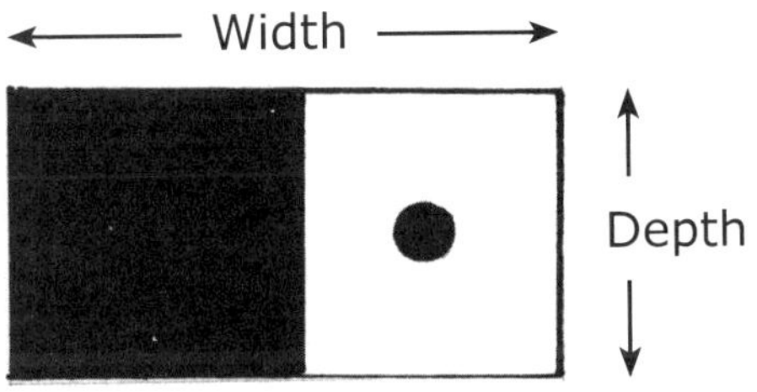

FIGURE 1

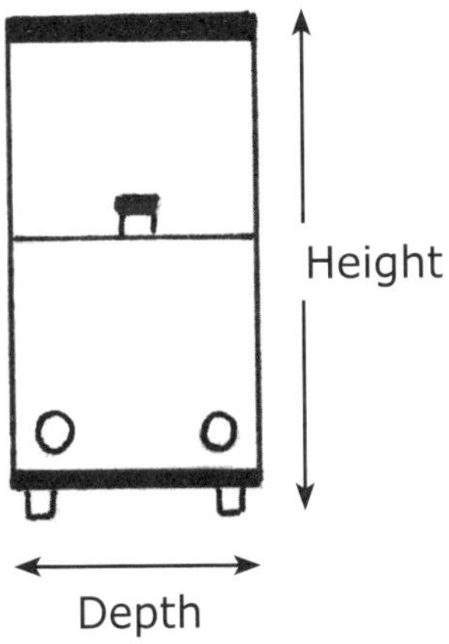

FIGURE 2

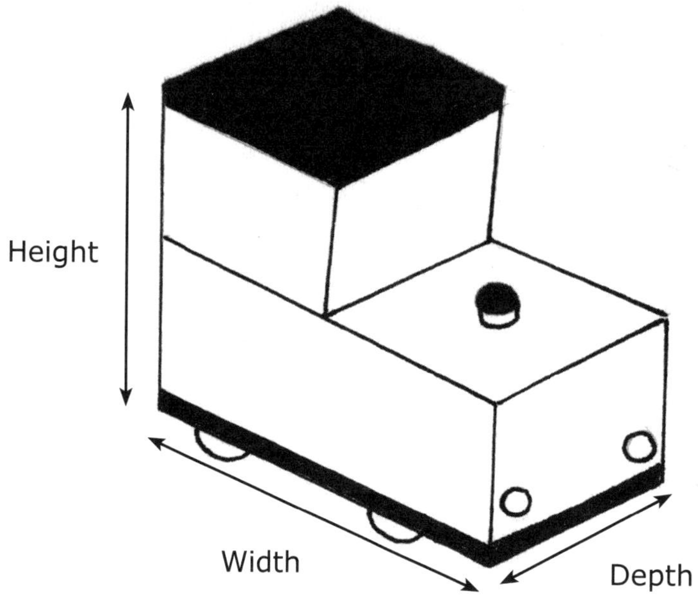

FIGURE 3

Imagine the letter A turning little by little to the top view, front view, right-side view, and bottom view.

Top View

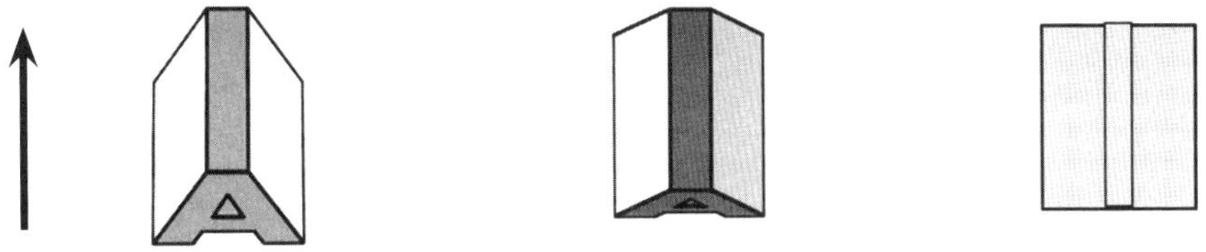

Front View

Right-Side View

Bottom View

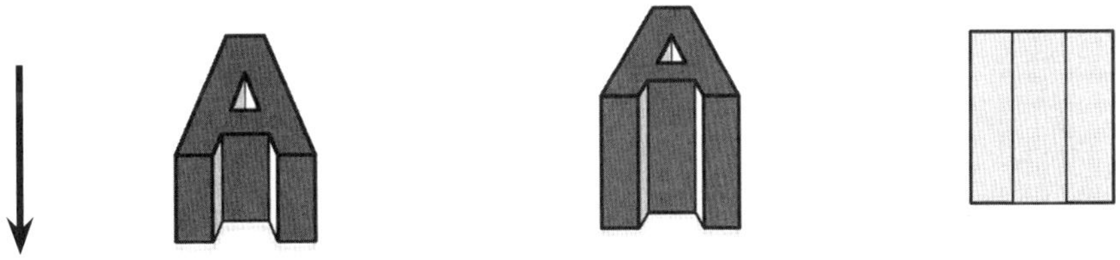

Challenge 1: Hiding Ladybugs

Stickman and his two pet ladybugs (Zebra and Dots) are playing around the 3-D letters.

1. Draw the top view and the front view of the letter and Stickman.

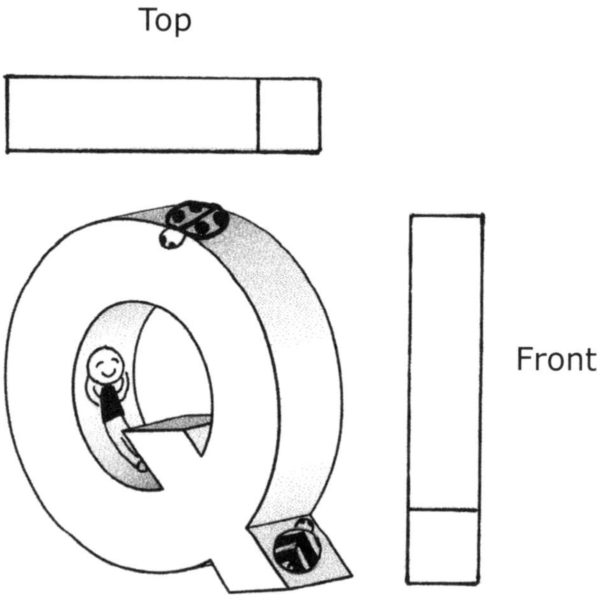

2. Draw the ladybugs and Stickman.

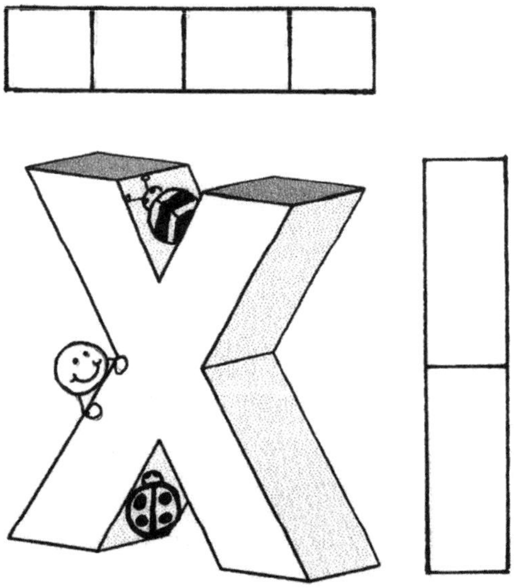

Challenge 2: Where Can They Hide?

Mark with an X the places where the ladybugs can hide from people looking at them from the top view of each letter. Then mark where they can hide from the right-side view of each letter.

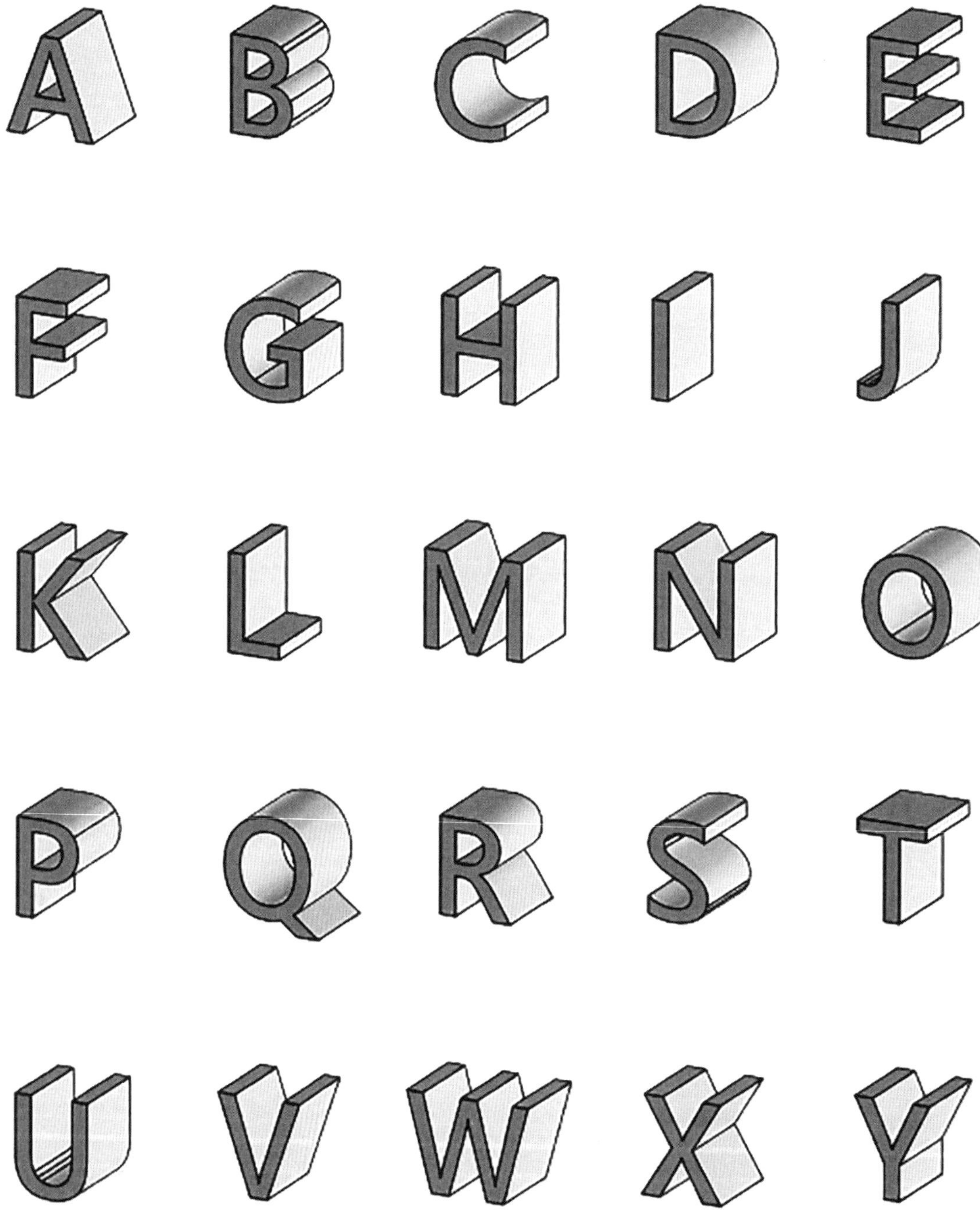

Challenge 3: 3-D Lines

These are 3-D chairs. A few changes in the lines make a different view.

Draw someone sitting in each chair. Would you look at their back, side, or front?

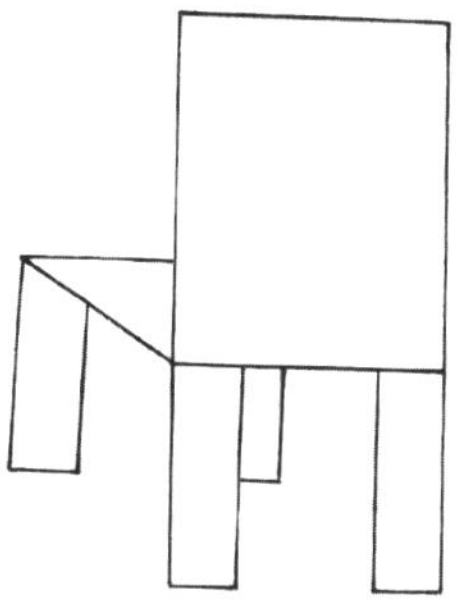
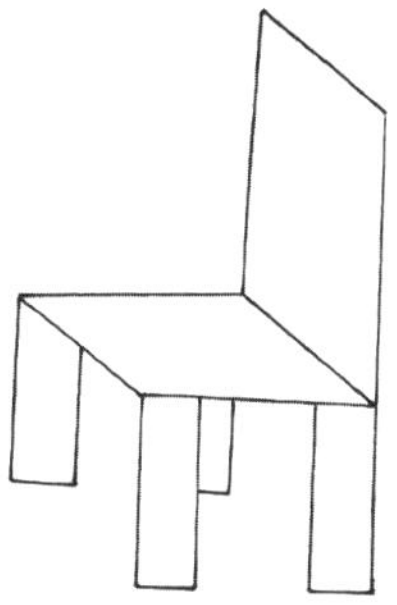
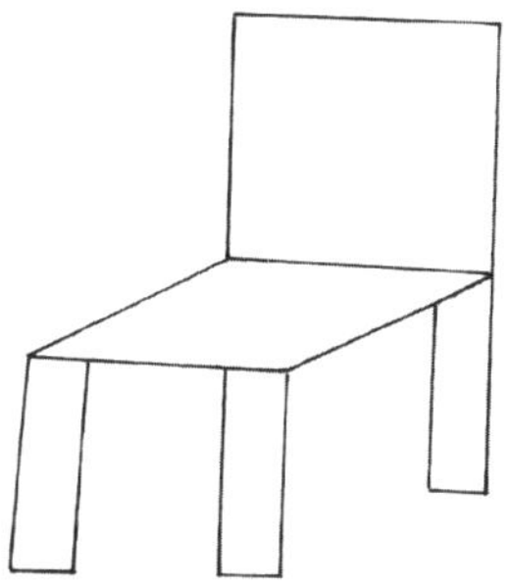
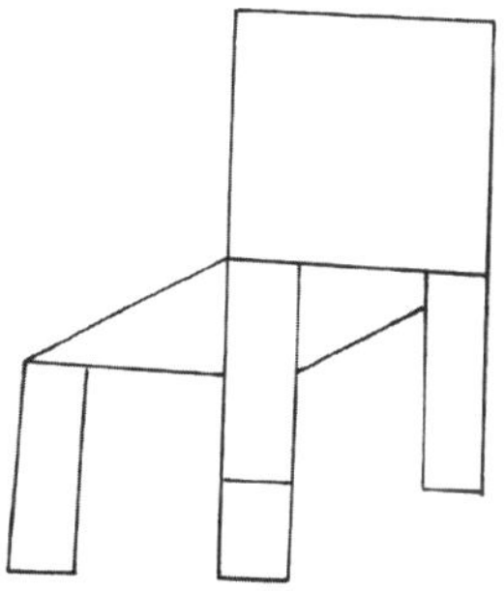

These are 3-D stairs.

Draw someone climbing the stairs.

Sometimes the lines are used incorrectly and the shape does not look right.

Make the wrong lines disappear by using black to color the shapes to make them look right.

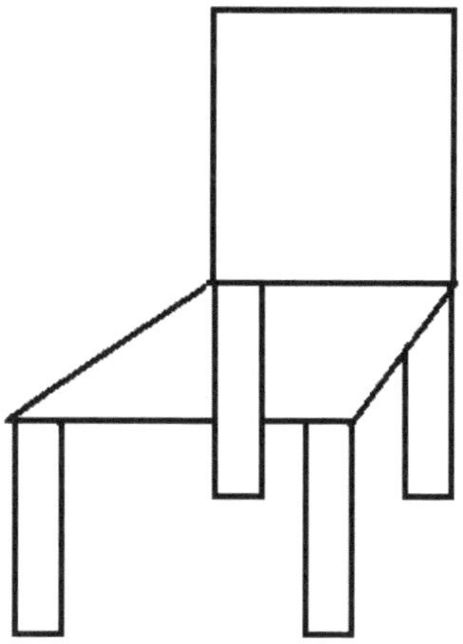

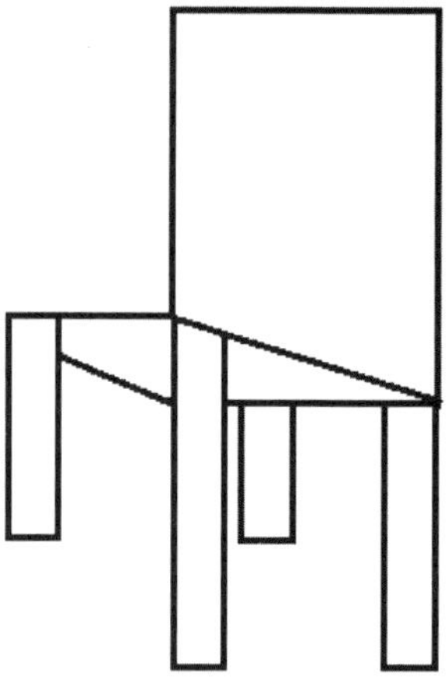

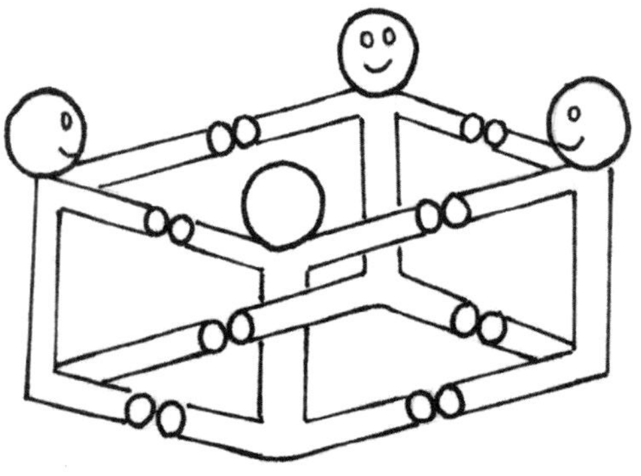

Challenge 4: 3-D Shading

Shading helps to set off some parts of a shape. Below is a picture of three mugs: one empty, one full of milk, and one upside down.

Which cup do you think is full of milk? Shade the empty mug so it looks full of milk.

Empty Mug

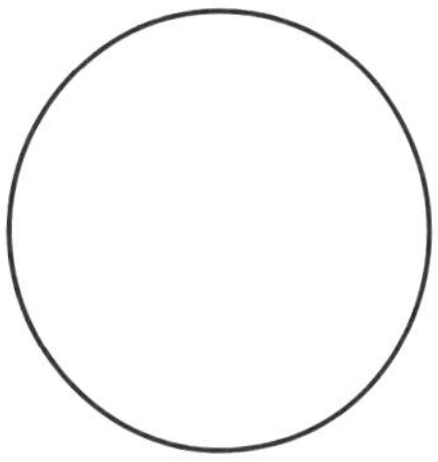

These 3-D shapes are similar but Shape 1 has a flat center and Shape 2 has a hole. The top view of the two figures is the same, but shading would help to make clear which top view belongs to which shape.

Shade the top view for Shape 1 to show a flat center and the top view for Shape 2 to show a hole.

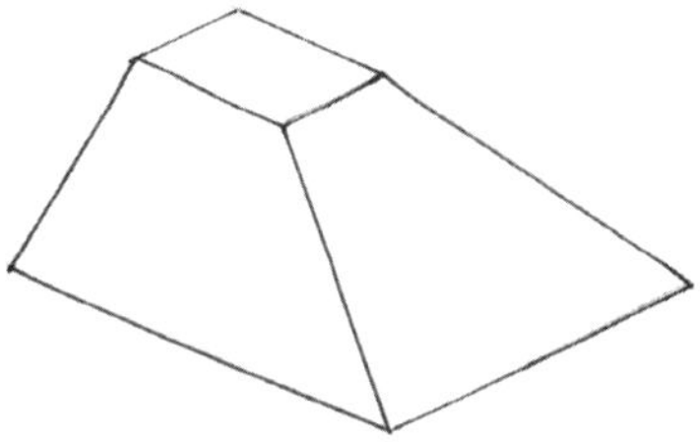

Shape 1

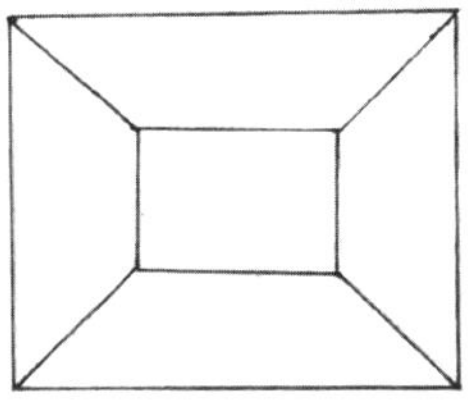

Top View

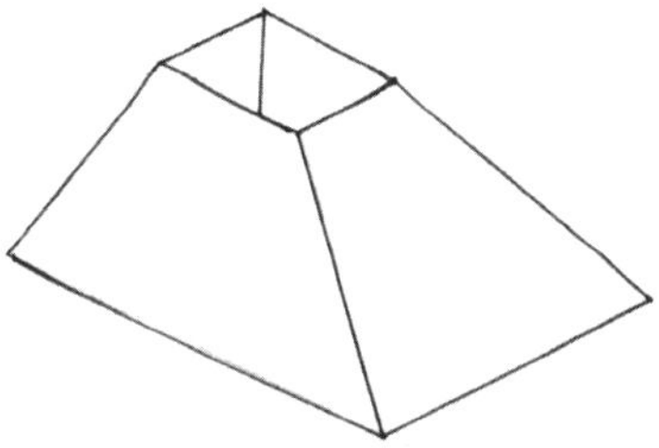

Shape 2

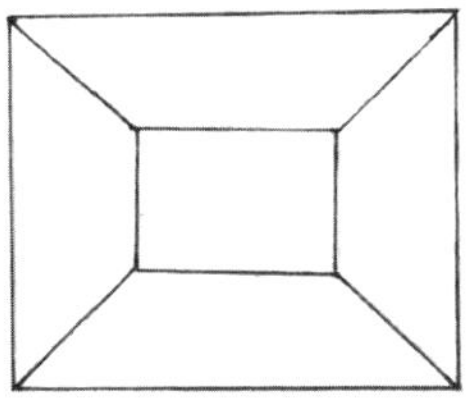

Top View

Challenge 5: Perspective of Cups and Coins

Perspective is how things look in comparison with other things.

Below are two cups exactly the same size. The one on the left looks bigger because it is closer to the camera. It is actually on top of another cup.

The farthest cup looks so small it fits inside the handle of the closest cup.

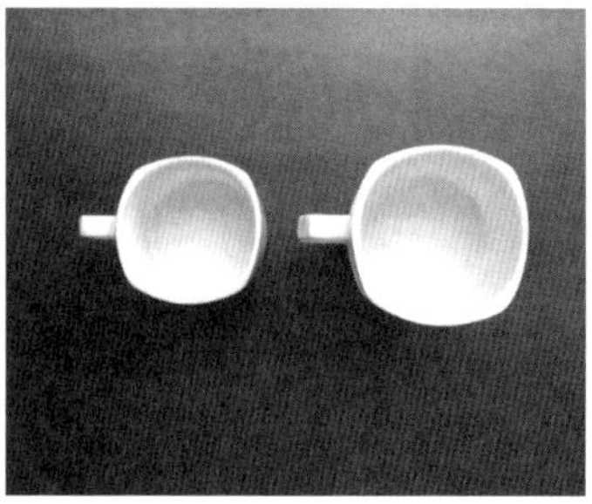

1. Look for different objects to show perspective.

2. Take three coins of the same size. Put two of them on the floor one right next to the other. Take the third coin between your fingers and close one eye.

   Look to see if the coin in your hand can cover the view of the two coins on the floor. How many coins placed together on the floor can the coin block from your view when you are standing? How many when you are kneeling?

   Look for bigger circular objects and see if the coin can still block their view.

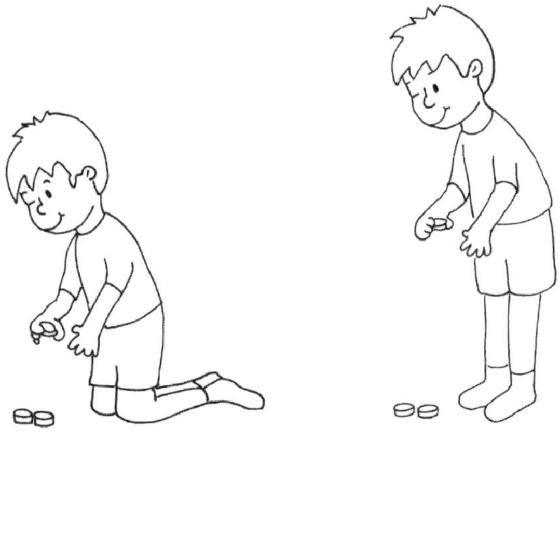

3. Take a flashlight and place it in front of a coin. Look how the shadow grows when the light and coin get farther from the ground.

The shadow of the coin blocks the view of the circular object at the same height when you can no longer see the object under the coin.

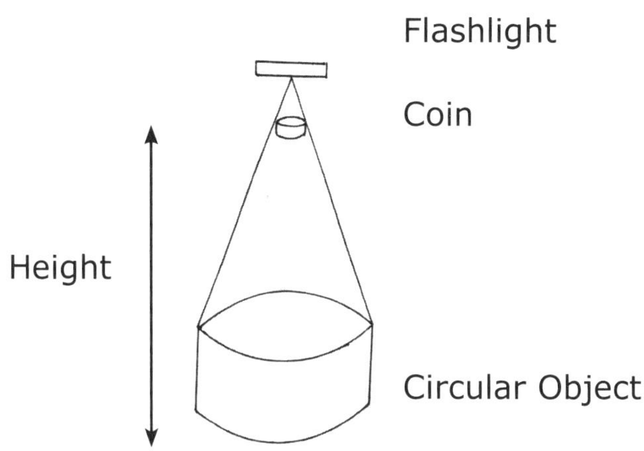

4. Do different experiments. Place on the floor different sizes of objects on the floor to see where they are blocked from your view.

Challenge 6: 2-D Shading

Play with shading 2-D figures to learn how it works.

There are five figures to cut out on page 189. Cut them inside the line.

1. Take figure 1 and place the shaded rectangle where it is indicated and use tape to make it stick. Lift the figure up like in this photo.

   Use your cell phone flashlight. Place it on Board 1 behind the light line. Move the cell phone until your shade matches the shadow line (a line that goes from the side of the figure to the flashlight) in figure 1.

   Move the flashlight to one side until the shadow matches the parallel line in figure 1. Look how the shadow line at the other side of the figure has widened.

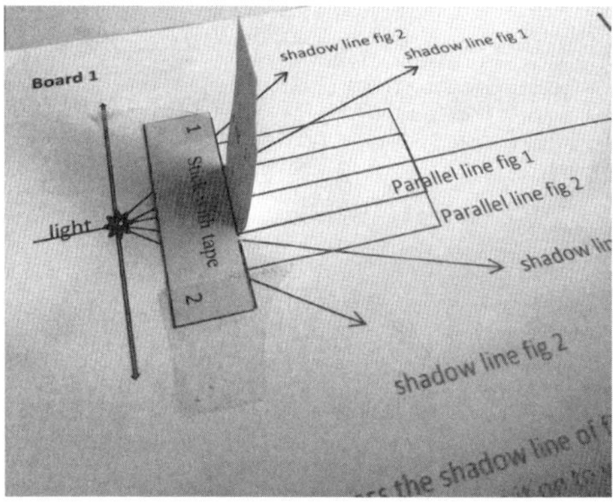

2. Do the same with figure 2. Stick it on top of figure 1.

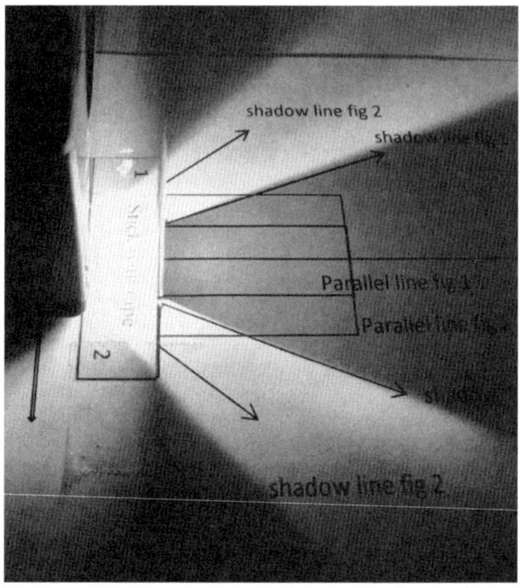

3. Draw the shadow line for figure 3 before turning on the light. Turn on the light and find out if you were right.

4. Repeat with figures 4 and 5.

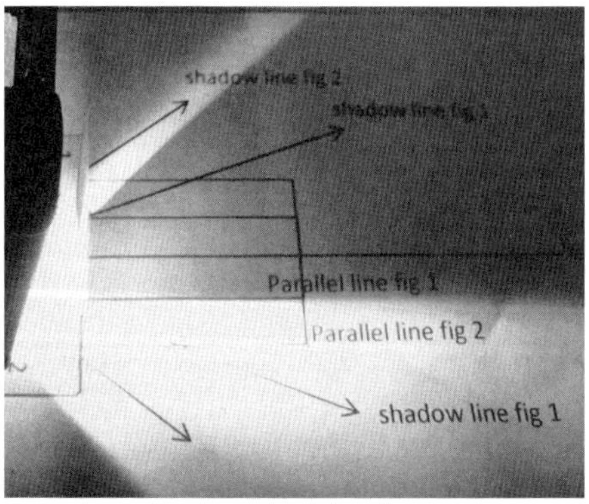

5. Lift the flashlight up (using the same shadow line but higher) and look how the shadow becomes smaller.

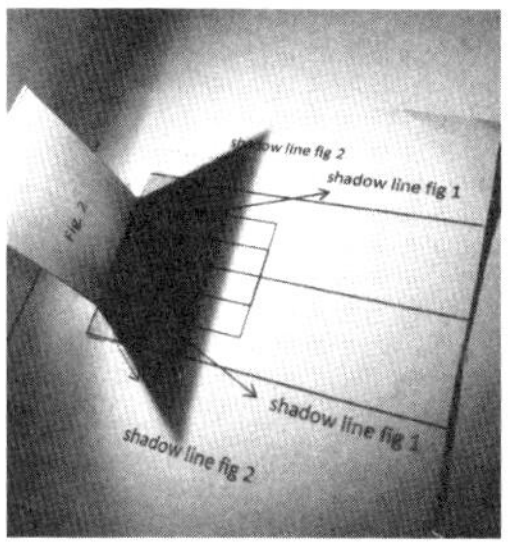

There is an imaginary line from the flashlight that passes to the highest point of the figure and ends on the farthest area of the shadow.

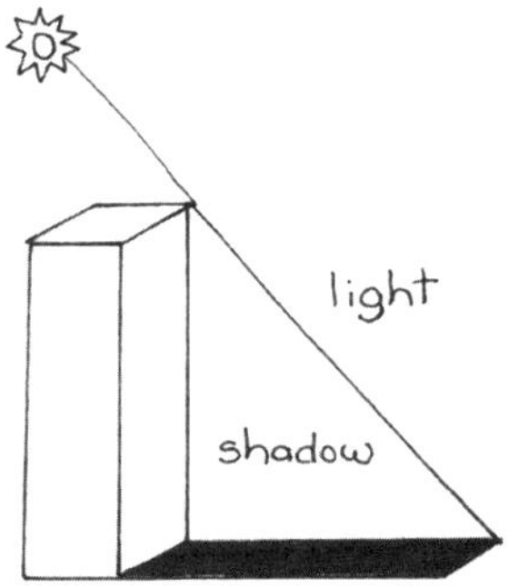

The more you lift the light, the smaller the shadow gets.

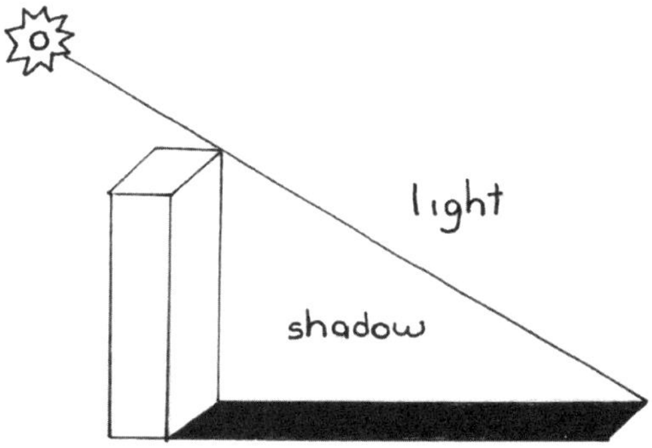

6. Cut different figures from paper, stick them on with tape, and look the different shadows. Move the light far or up.

What did you find out?

____

____

____

7. Now use Board 2 on page 191. Cut different figures until you get a shadow that matches. You can lift the light. Glue the figure that matches below.

8. For Board 3 on page 191, make a triangle that matches the shade. You can lift the flashlight from the floor but the flashlight should not be at the center of the figure. Glue the figure that matches.

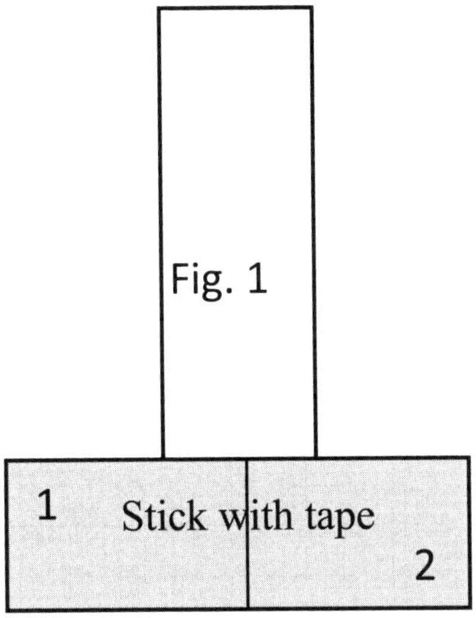
Fig. 1
1
Stick with tape
2

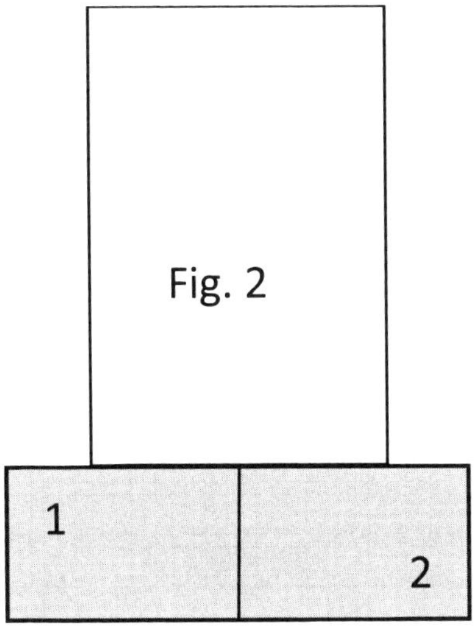
Fig. 2
1
2

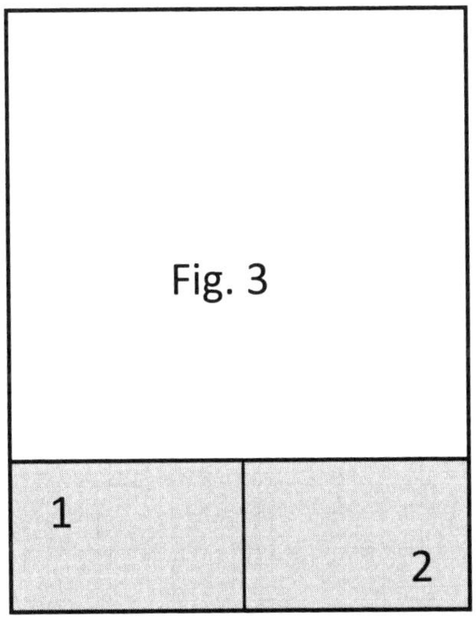
Fig. 3
1
2

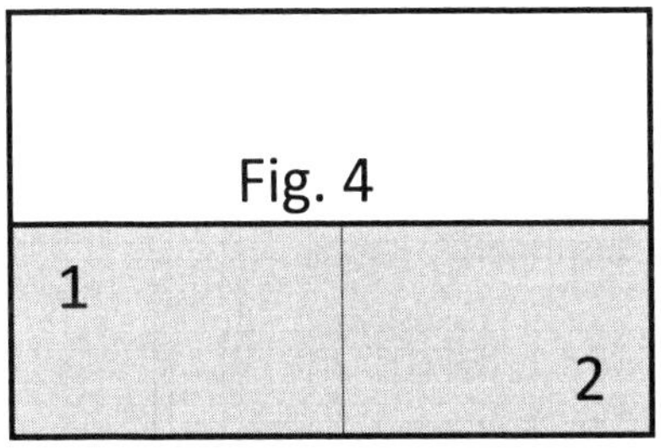
Fig. 4
1
2

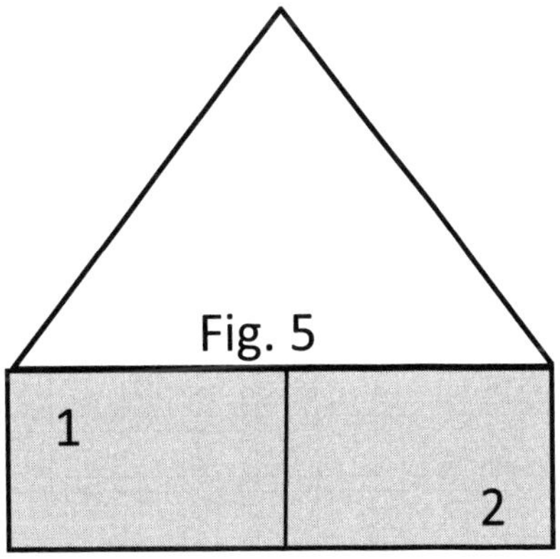
Fig. 5
1
2

Board 1

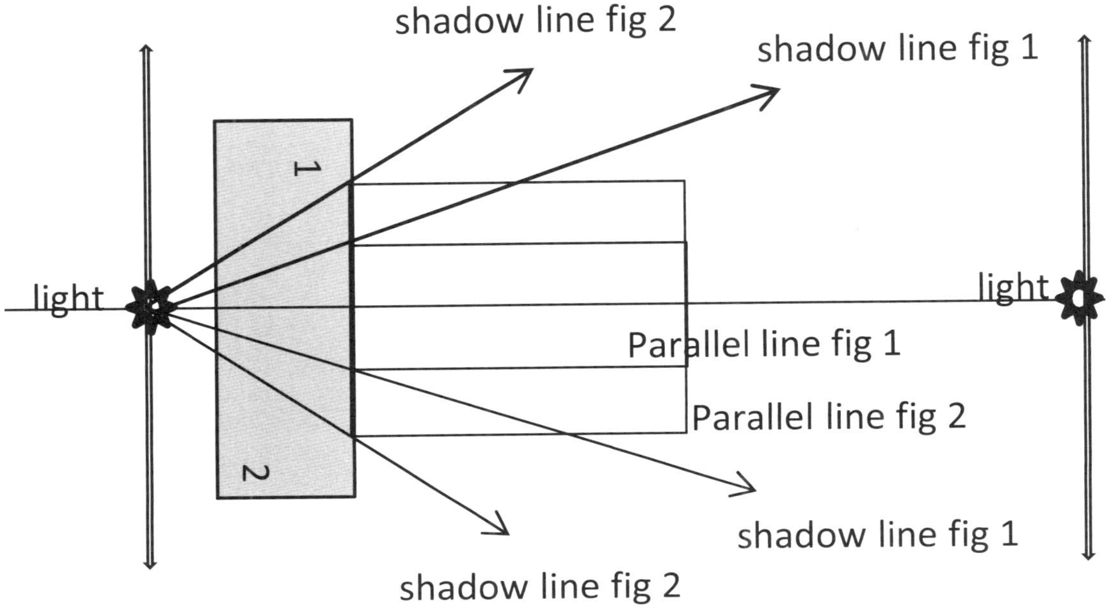

Challenge: Guess the shadow line of figures 3, 4 , 5 with the light off. Then turn it on to verify.

Board 2

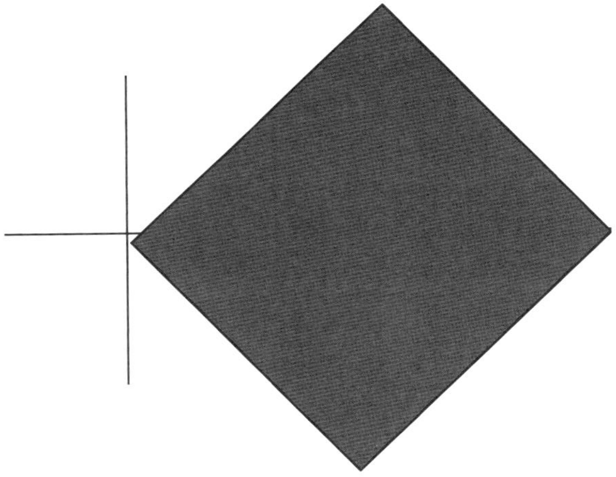

Challenge: Find the figure that can make this shade in this position

Board 3

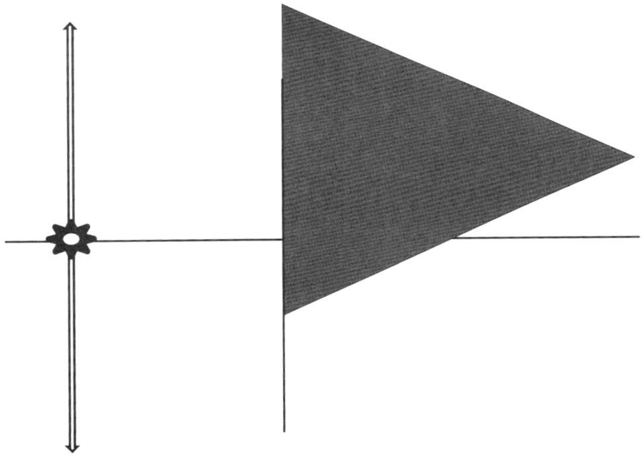

Challenge: Find the figure that can make a triangle like this when it is not at the center of the light

Challenge 7: Making 3-D Cube Patterns

1. How would you make a paper cube?

You could cut a pattern of 4 squares and fold it.

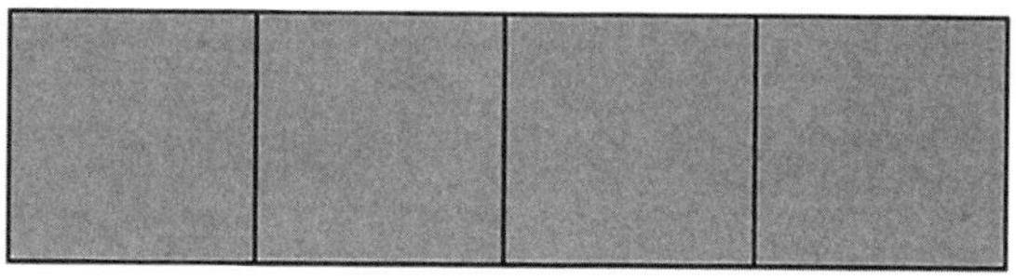

Then cut two squares, one for the top and one for the bottom, and glue them on.

2. How would you make a cube with a continuous pattern?

The following are examples of patterns that form a cube.

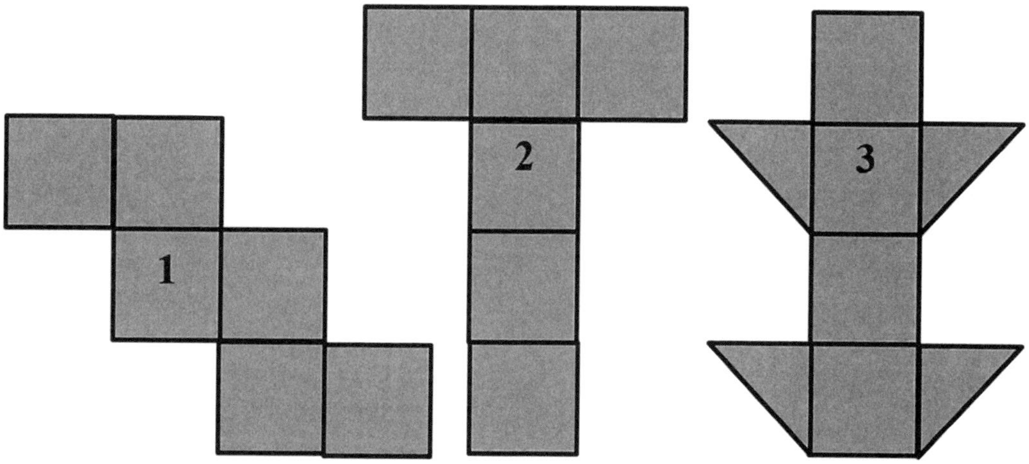

1. Now make your own patterns. Cut out the patterns and fold them to make a cube. Make all the different patterns you can, but do not repeat the same pattern in different positions. For example, do not draw pattern 2 upside down. Use the grid on the next page to experiment.

Challenge: Make 20 different patterns. You can use separate sheets of paper.

2. The grid below is 5 squares wide by 6 squares long. How many cube patterns can you fit in the grid? You can use more than one pattern. Draw your patterns by placing them in different positions.

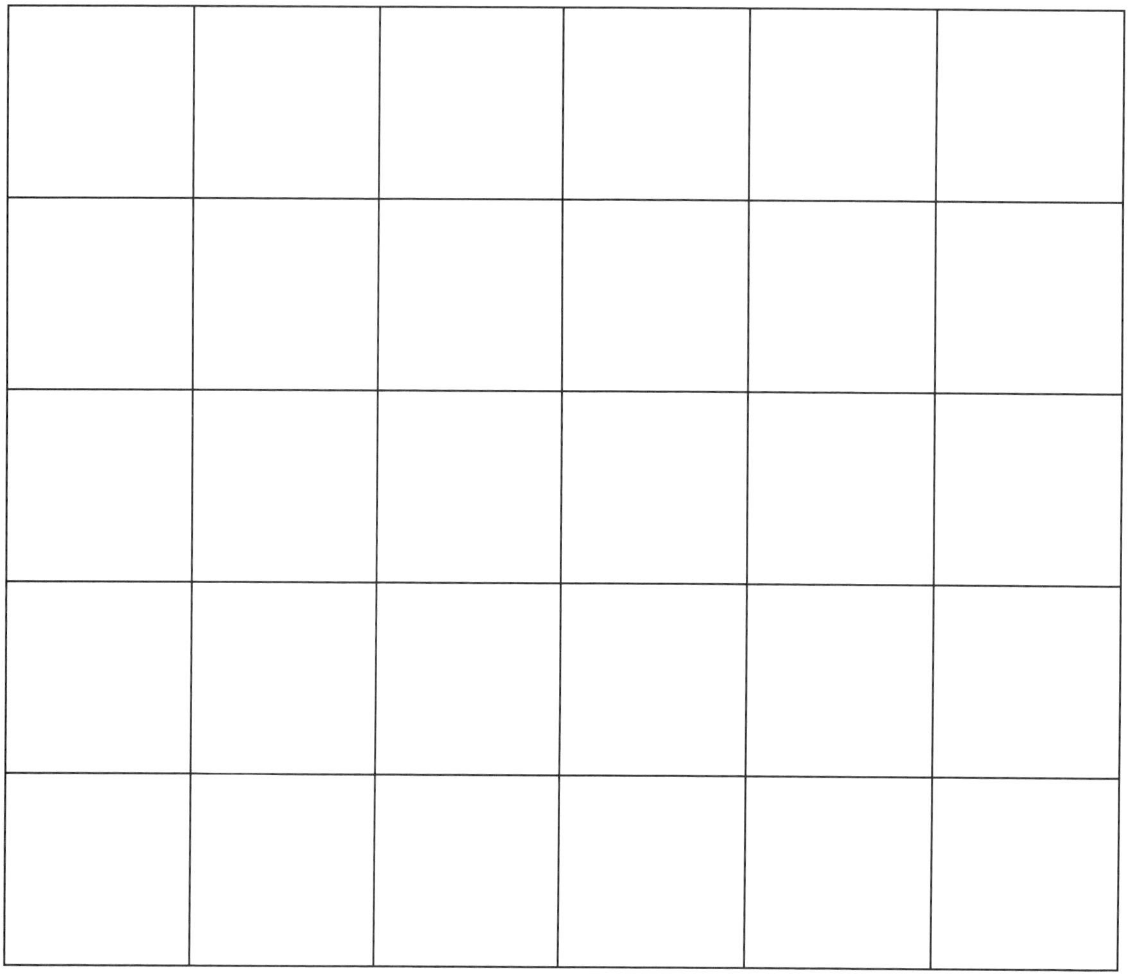

For example:

3 Cubes Using One Pattern

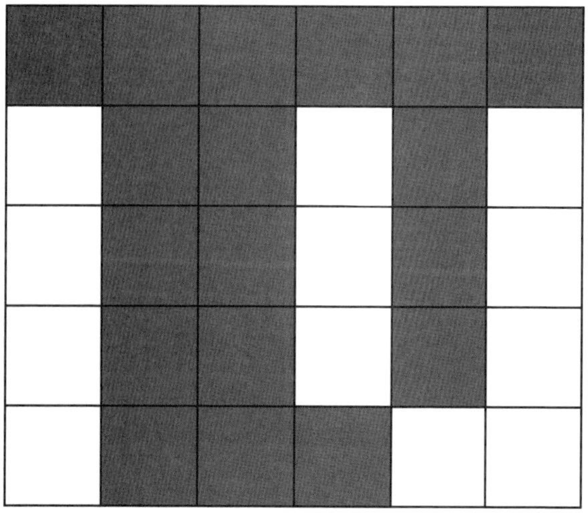

3 Cubes Using Two Patterns

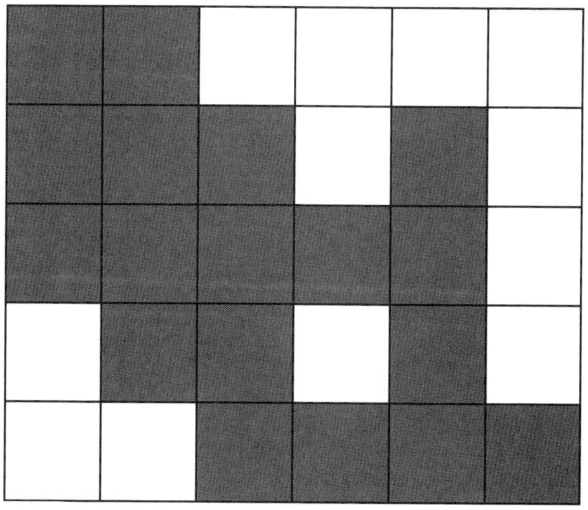

Challenge: Draw 4 patterns in a square grid of 6 x 5. Here are practice grids.

Challenge 8: Making Ball Patterns

Imagine you make different types of balls from plastic sheets. How would you make them?

Look at different kind of balls to figure out the patterns they are made from.

1. Draw the pattern of one of the pieces the balls are made of. How many pieces is used to make each ball?

Baseball Pattern ______ Pieces	Soccer Ball Pattern _____ Pieces
Beach Ball Pattern ______ Pieces	**Basketball Pattern _____ Pieces**

If you have to fit all the patterns needed to make one ball on a single sheet of paper, which of the patterns will make it easier? Make a pattern for a ball the size of an orange and try to fit some together in the square below.

Baseball	**Soccer**
Beach Ball	**Basketball**

2. If all the balls were the size of an orange, which one would you prefer to make? Why?

____

____

____

Super Challenge

11. Play With Mechanisms

A mechanism is a system of parts that work together in a machine.

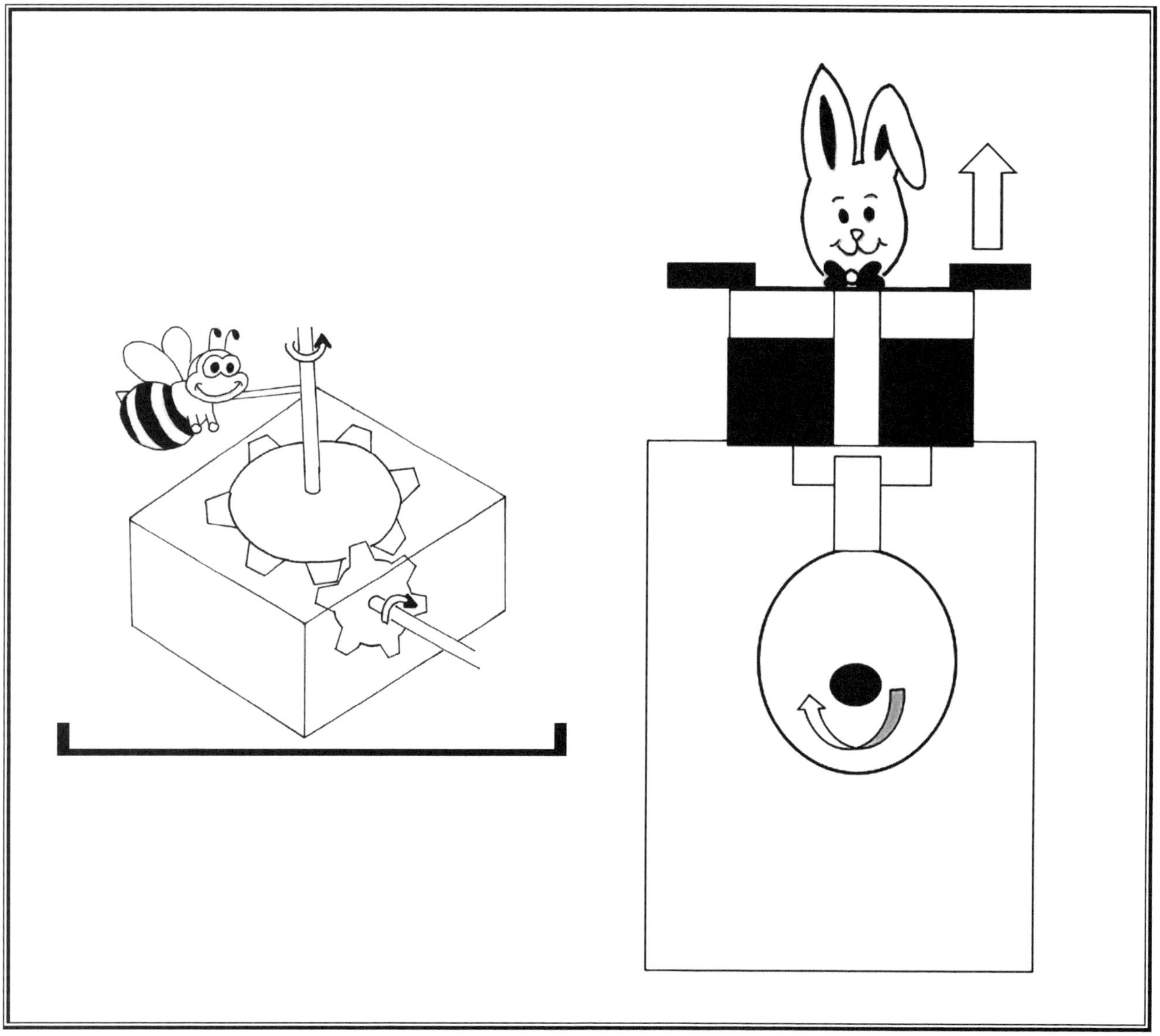

Example: Pop-Up Rabbit With a Cam Mechanism

A cam is a shape (disk or cylinder) fixed to a shaft. See the figure below. The shaft rotates, turning the cam. The cam pushes the follower up and down. The sliders keep the follower in its position and help it slide.

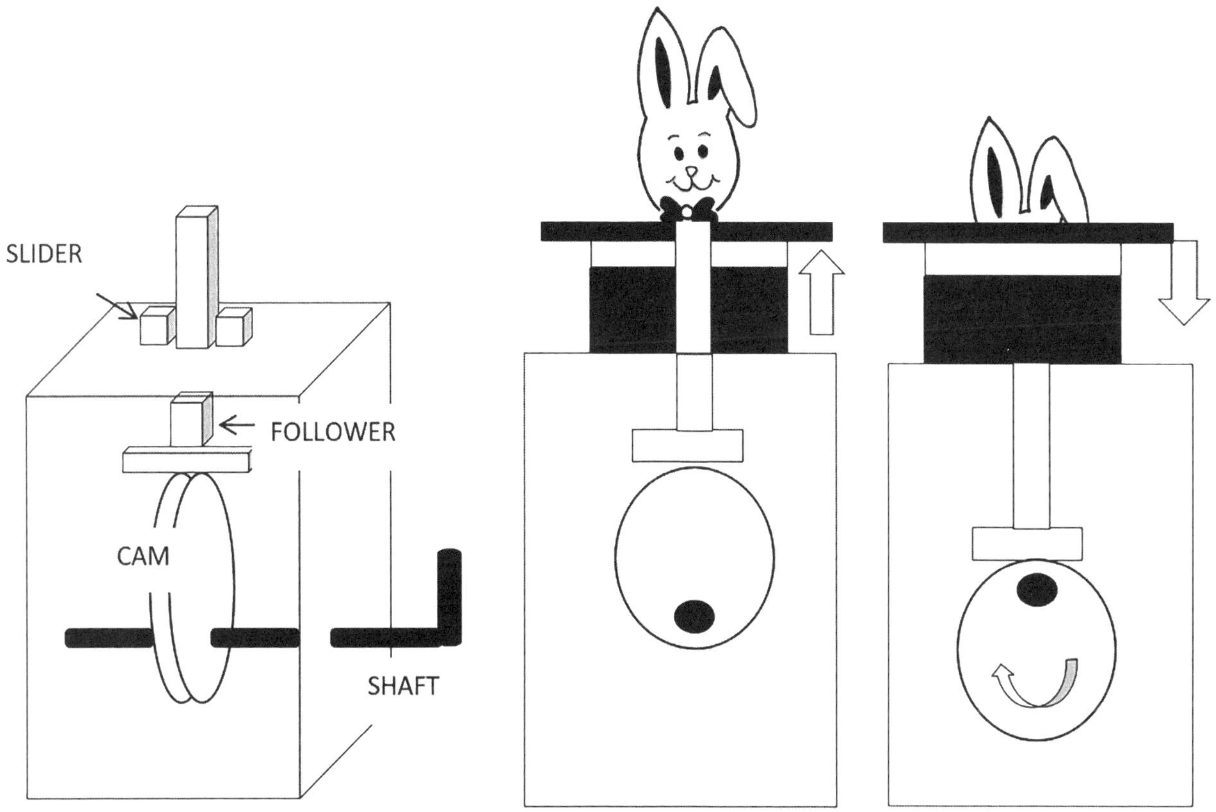

Below is the process to make a pop-up rabbit with a cam mechanism. There will be issues that you will need to solve.

1. First, look for materials. You need a small container with a lid that is easy to open, such as a small can of potato chips or a paper cup with a lid or something similar. The shaft will be a pencil and a piece of cardboard such as a notebook cover will be used to make the cam and follower. The patterns for the circle cam and follower are below.

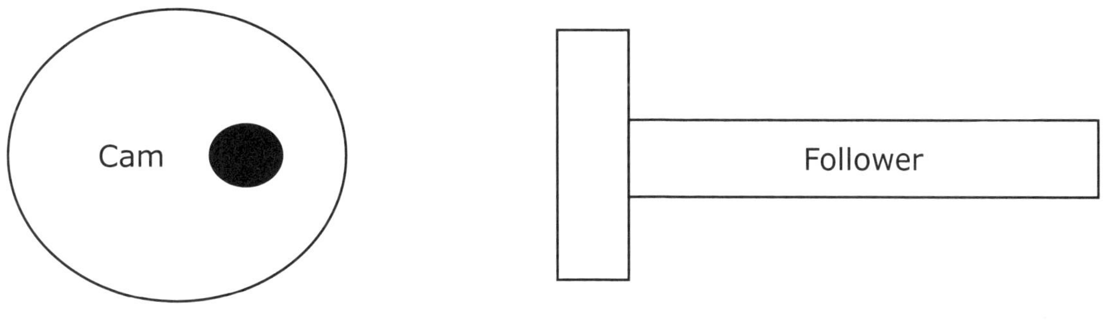

2. Place the cam outside the container and make a hole with a pen (the tip must be strong) where the cam will not touch the bottom. Continue to the other side of the can.

3. Insert a pencil in the hole and turn it to check if the cam hits the bottom or the sides of the container.

4. Make a hole in the lid with a pen and extended it with scissors to fit the follower. Insert the follower. Turn the pencil to find Issue 1.

Issue 1: The follower falls to the bottom when you turn the pencil.

Write or draw your ideas for possible solutions.

____

____

____

Example solutions: Use tape to narrow the hole where the follower is placed or change the follower. Make a slot to the follower to help it stay over the cam or change the design of the follower.

Test the solutions: The tape to narrow the lid hole helped a little, but if the hole is very small the follower does not move, and if it gets bigger the follower falls.

The slot to the follower did not help.

Maybe a follower that cannot fall needs to be almost as big as the lid.

Make a cardboard circle, glue it, and tape it to an ice cream stick. Did this work?

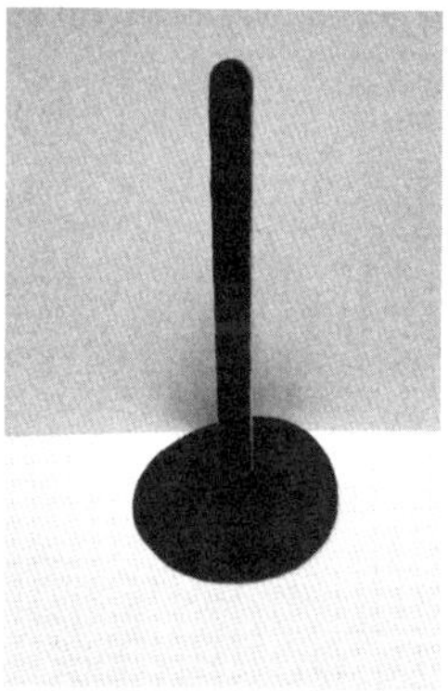

Issue 2: The follower circle is so big it sticks to the sides of the can. The stick did not slide smoothly at the lid.

Write or draw your ideas for possible solutions.

Example solutions: Make the follower circle smaller. Also make a new slider. (It is quite obvious that a hole and tape is not a good work for a slider.)

Test the solutions: The smaller circle works much better. Now it is time to focus on the slider.

Use cardboard that can be easily folded. Make four triangles. Tape two triangles on the top of the lid looking north and south and tape two on the bottom looking east and west.

Make a paper rabbit and paste it to the follower. Make a hat and paste it to the lid. Try your pop-up rabbit to find another issue.

Issue 3: You have a shy rabbit. It does not pop all the way up. Also it does not pop up every time the pencil is turned.

The cam does not stay on the center of the pencil (it is not glued to the pencil). Also the pencil keeps sliding to one side or the other of the container which also makes the cam not stay on center.

Write or draw your ideas for possible solutions.

____

____

____

Example solutions: Make the stick follower bigger by adding cardboard. Also glue the cam to the pencil. (This will make the container stay at the center of the pencil). We cannot glue the pencil to the cam because then it will not roll. Instead, put tape on both sides of the pencil to make it stay in the same place.

Test the solutions: The tape works fine.

Here is your first pop-up rabbit with a cam mechanism.

There are many mechanisms which can make an object go up and down like the cam mechanism.

Write or draw your plans for a different mechanism. You could use a paper cup with a lid and straw.

Challenge 1: Flying Bee With a Gear Mechanism

A gear is a wheel with teeth that has different uses. Two uses are shown below.

Change the Speed of a Gear

The smaller gear turns faster than the bigger gear.

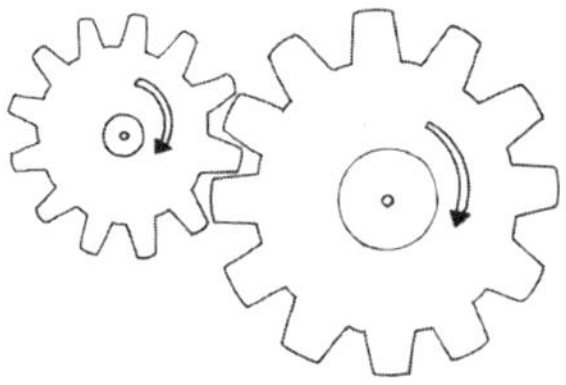

Change the Direction of the Motion

A gear turns on the side making the gear at the top turn too.

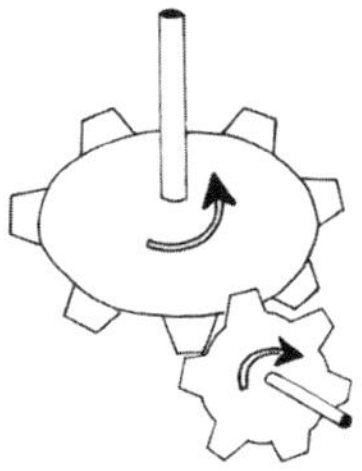

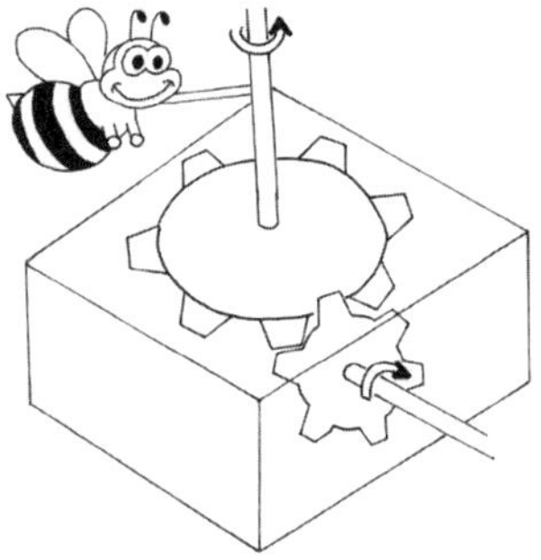

Below is a process to make a flying bee with a gear mechanism. There will be issues that you will have to solve.

1. First, look for materials. You need a small cardboard box with a lid, a stick for the shaft, and a piece of cardboard such as a notebook cover to make the gears.

Make two cardboard gears with the pattern to the right. The gear is small because your box is small too.

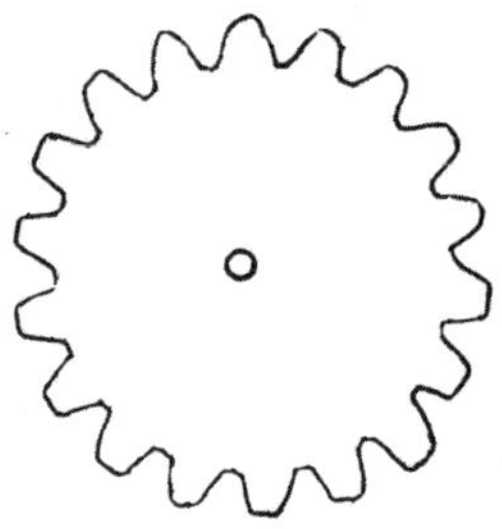

2. Make the holes on the sides of the box using the tip of the stick.

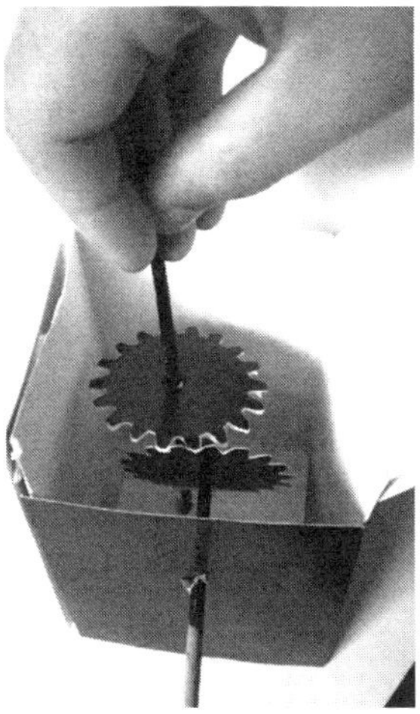

3. Verify that the side gear turns and place the top gear next to it to know where to make the bottom hole.

4. Turn the side gear and when the top gear turns too, insert the stick on the bottom.

5. Remove the stick and insert the tip on the bottom side and continue inserting it up to make a hole on the box lid.

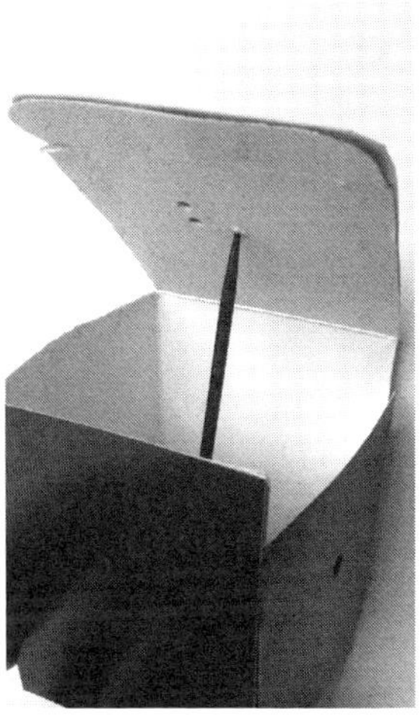

6. Make a couple of holes to make sure the stick stays straight up.

You learned in the example that the gears should be glued to the stick to prevent them from sliding. You also learned to put tape on the sides of the stick to avoid it from moving to the sides of the box.

7. Turn the side gear. The top gear turns but then stops. Make a hole in the side of the box to see what is happening and find Issue 1.

Issue 1: The teeth of the side gear have moved down the teeth of the top gear. Even if you put them in the right place, it kept happening. The gear material is soft so it does not help it to stay still.

Write or draw your ideas for possible solutions.

Example solution: Change the design of the gear to make your flying bee with a gear mechanism.

Think if fewer or more teeth will be better or if larger or smaller teeth will help.

Challenge 2: Toy Car or Ball Launcher

The ball or car comes off the launcher and moves a few inches forward.

Look for a small ball or toy car (or make a paper ball or launch an eraser).

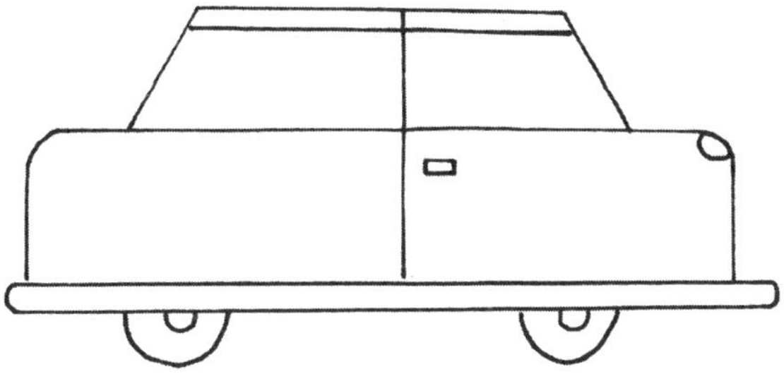

Draw your plans for a mechanism to launch your ball or car. Do one using a sliding box as shown below.

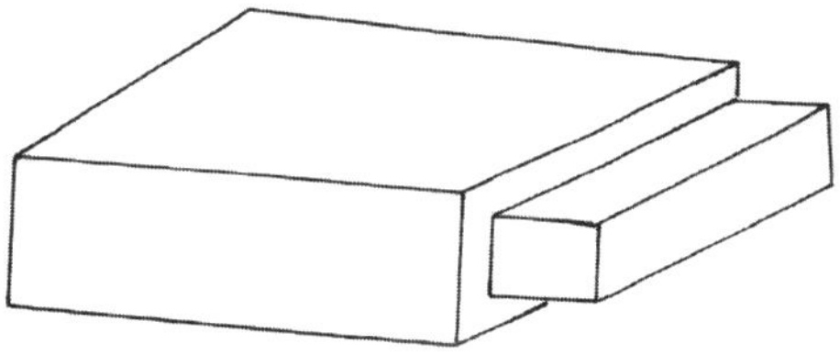

Challenge 3: Car Driven by Rubber Bands

You are going to make a simple car driven by rubber bands. Then you will make changes to its design to make it better.

1. Take two ice cream sticks and glue them together on one end. Take one straw and cut it into three parts and glue them to the sticks as shown. (The straws are black in the picture). Cut a stick and insert it into the straws.

2. Use four bottle caps for the wheels. Make a hole in each one.

3. Take two rubber bands and cut one to make a string and make a knot to tie it to the stick (rear side of the car). Make a knot in the other rubber band. Use the second rubber band to tie it to the front part of the car.

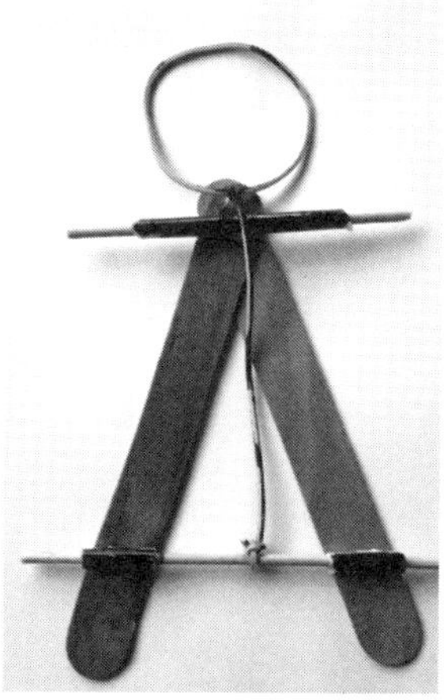

4. Insert the caps onto the sticks. Glue just one cap to each stick to make it possible to take the stick off for later wheel changes. (You can use tape or Play-Doh to make the second wheel tide if needed.)

5. The car works by rolling the back wheels to make the rubber band tight. (If it does not get tight, try putting a rubber band around the wheels.)

Now test the speed of the car. Choose an exit point and use a chronometer to measure the time it takes to get to a different point.

Write the time it took. ________________________

1. Does the car move straight ahead or go to the side? Did you see any problems?

____

____

____

2. How do you think you could make your car faster?

____

____

____

3. Do you think smaller or larger wheels will make it faster? Why?

____

____

____

4. Look on the Internet for information about the size of the wheels and speed. What did you find out?

____

____

____

5. Do you think a wider or thinner wheel will make it faster? Why?

____

____

____

6. Look on the Internet information about the width of the wheels and speed. What did you find out?

____

____

____

7. Change your wheels. You can make many changes. For example, put large can lids on the back and two bottle caps on the front.

a. Measure again the speed using the same exit and arriving point.

Write the time it took. ______________________

b. Compare the time with the previous one. Is it better or worse?

____

8. Is there a different way to use the rubber band or to add bands? How do you think a smaller or thinner band will affect the result?

____

____

____

9. Write ideas for a different car or for changing the one you have.

____

____

____

a. Test your new car.

Write the time it took. ______________________

b. Compare it with the first and second time. Write your conclusions.